Germany Through American Eyes

Published in cooperation with
The Robert Bosch Foundation, GmbH,
and
The Robert Bosch Foundation Alumni Association

Germany Through American Eyes

Foreign Policy and Domestic Issues

edited by Gale A. Mattox
and John H. Vaughan, Jr.

To D. Davis

Gene

Westview Press
BOULDER, SAN FRANCISCO, & LONDON

Copyright © 1989 by Westview Press, Inc.

Published in 1989 in the United States of America by Westview Press, Inc., 5500 Central Avenue, Boulder, Colorado 80301, and in the United Kingdom by Westview Press, Inc., 13 Brunswick Centre, London WC1N 1AF, England

Library of Congress Cataloging-in-Publication Data
Germany through American eyes.
  Includes index.
  1. Germany (West)—Foreign relations. 2. Germany
(West)—Social conditions. 3. Germany (West)—Economic
conditions. 4. Germany (East)—Foreign relations.
I. Mattox, Gale A. II. Vaughan, John H., Jr., 1951–
DD258.8.G47 1989   327.43   88-37859
ISBN 0-8133-0769-4

Printed and bound in the United States of America

The paper used in this publication meets the requirements of the American National
Standard for Permanence of Paper for Printed Library Materials Z39.48-1984.

10   9   8   7   6   5   4   3   2   1

Contents

Foreword

Although international understanding can be practiced in many ways, it is not possible without an accurate knowledge of other cultures, including the personal experience of living in foreign countries.

The problems of our time have national, transnational, even global elements. We must therefore continue to develop the consciousness that these problems—between East and West, North and South—can only be solved through the lasting understanding that transcends daily politics. Such an understanding is based on the mutual knowledge of our various lifestyles and visions of the future.

The objective of the Robert Bosch Foundation, a private philanthropic establishment, is to help secure the future for succeeding generations on the North American and European continents and in our two countries, the United States and the Federal Republic of Germany (FRG). To this end the foundation wants to contribute with the resources at its disposal. The foundation sees its promotion of information, knowledge of foreign languages, and cultural comparisons (which will have a geometric effect in the future) as one of its most important tasks.

Since 1984 the Robert Bosch Foundation has annually invited fifteen young, highly qualified Americans to a nine-month stay in the FRG. The foundation conceived the program and carries it out under its own auspices.

The selection of the participants follows a rigorous screening process. The applicants do not have to know German beforehand, but immediately after selection they receive stipends to learn German or to improve their knowledge of it while still in the United States. For a successful stay in Germany, working and living in everyday German society, a good knowledge of the language is indispensable.

Bosch Fellows in the FRG work at high levels in federal and regional establishments, businesses and banks, administrative bodies, television and radio stations, and on newspapers. They deal with current political, economic, and cultural problems—in Berlin with East-West relations, in Brussels with the development of the European Community and NATO, and in Paris with intra-European cooperation from the French perspective. The Fellows get to know Germany and Europe "from the inside" in the course of their active participation in their respective professional areas. Based on these intensive experiences, they write reports with themes of their own choosing. The publication of many of these works, above all in professional journals, attests to their quality.

The program is an example of the Robert Bosch Foundation's self-perception. The foundation conceives of its activities for the common good as a business undertaking. It not only sets the conditions for its financial support of philanthropic projects but also conceptualizes and develops its own programs to give reality to its policies. This applies to all the spheres in which it is active—health matters, general welfare, cultural and educational affairs, and, most importantly, to international understanding with an emphasis on German-French, German-Polish, and German-U.S. relations.

The rapid success of the program is manifested in the decision of the first group of Bosch Fellows to found an alumni association. The association has already been very active and organizes an ever-growing annual alumni conference, which has been held in both Washington and New York.

Together with the Alumni Association, the Robert Bosch Foundation has decided to establish a series of books in which the best reports are published. The authors themselves are responsible for the contents. The Robert Bosch Foundation wishes the series and its authors every success and hopes that this book and succeeding ones will contribute to German-U.S. understanding.

Peter Payer
Executive Director
The Robert Bosch Foundation

Preface

As scholars and writers have attested throughout the years, Germany can be a fascinating as well as challenging country in which to study and live. Its geopolitical position in Central Europe has given it significant influence over the course of European history. It has been a country of contradictions and of momentous events that have had tremendous impact on the international community.

For the U.S. Fellows in the Robert Bosch Foundation Fellow Program there may be as many reasons for participation in the program as there are Fellows. Whereas some came from German-American families, others had only a cursory knowledge of the country. The interests of some Fellows was in German history or culture; others came to learn about business, industry, law, or other sectors of modern German life. Although the language competency of the participants varied initially, as did their knowledge of the country, the experience of the program had the universal effect of deepening their understanding of Germany and its people.

The program's objective—to give young U.S. professionals experience in German government and industry at an early point in their careers—is unique in a number of ways. It is the only German-U.S. program designed specifically for professionals from a broad range of occupations, with the objective of integrating them, at least for a short time, into German professional life. For German business and government, this has often been a novel approach. From the participants' point of view, it has been a successful program and a significant contribution to an understanding of their counterparts in Germany. In turn, their German counterparts have had the opportunity to broaden their knowledge of the United States through the Bosch Fellows. The longer-term impact of the program on German-U.S. relations has been more difficult to assess and may be better left to later generations. The Robert Bosch Foundation Alumni Association has undertaken to further the goal of U.S.-German relations with this book.

Germany Through American Eyes

The reports selected for inclusion in *Germany Through American Eyes* represent the broad range of issue areas in which the Bosch Fellows were involved. They also reflect the varied viewpoints and interests of the Fellows, a strength of the program. Each chapter was selected as a contribution to the literature in the particular field. Although there was no attempt to be comprehensive and cover all of the Fellows' fields of endeavor, the selected chapters reflect the diverse interests of the participants in the program. The more than forty Fellows who traveled and lived in the Federal Republic of Germany during the first three years of the program represented a broad spectrum of interests and career paths, including law, business, academics, international banking and economics, chemistry, and journalism. Not only were the participants able to bring their wide-ranging experience and background to their German colleagues, but each participant also contributed to the general knowledge of their program colleagues.

The volume is organized into two parts—foreign policy and domestic policy—although the distinction is sometimes not so clear-cut. First, the comparative nature of some of the chapters means that even the most domestic issues have potential foreign policy implications. The discussions often transcend the traditional boundaries between domestic and foreign policy. Also, although the Bosch program is conducted in West Germany and West Berlin, many of the participants work in the Ministry for Inner-German Relations or in other areas of German-German affairs. The book deals primarily with West German affairs, but a number of chapters address the German Democratic Republic and its relations with the West. Hence, the book is truly about "Germany."

The chapters in Part One address some of the pressing German foreign policy issues in the postwar era. From different perspectives, they frame the challenges of the past and pose the dilemmas with which the future will confront us. In the opening chapter, Edwina S. Campbell discusses the transatlantic U.S.-German relationship since 1945, including its agreements as well as disagreements and misunderstandings. In a legal approach to the question of German-German relations, Kathryn S. Mack debates the vexing issue of East German recognition and the future of *Deutschlandpolitik*. Karin L. Johnston examines current changes in East German policy toward the Soviet Union and the West. Finally, Sandra E. Peterson addresses West German trade with the East during the 1980s and challenges some of the basic assumptions other scholars have made about German-German relations. Although the chapters do not cover all the issues and areas of German foreign policy, they give an overall impression of change amid public debate. The reader is left with a distinct feeling of an evolving German identity in foreign policy that will maintain its ties to the West but will become a more prominent world player, particularly within the European Community and in its relations with the East.

The chapters in Part Two survey a number of issues more domestic in nature, but not without international impact. Two of them—unemployment in West Germany and the environmental conditions for innovation in German industry—deal with problems of general concern in the industrialized world. Daniel J. Broderick reviews the West German political and economic approaches to the issue of unemployment, as well as possible remedies. David R. Larrimore looks at the structural problems plaguing German industry in the fast-growing field of high technology.

Barbara A. Reeves and A. Bradley Shingleton review issues on which very little comparative writing or in-depth research has been done. Discussion of Reeves's topic—the legal situation of battered women in the Federal Republic of Germany—was all but taboo until recent years, and there has been only limited comparative research on the subject. Thus, her work in this area on both sides of the Atlantic is of interest to both U.S. and German readers. Shingleton's chapter on document production is instructive both to the international lawyer interested in the intricacies of the German legal system and to the layperson interested in the different approaches to law in the two societies. Finally, Dennis P. McLaughlin focuses on the process of plea bargaining in the Federal Republic of Germany from the perspective of a U.S. attorney familiar with the process on this side of the Atlantic.

Appendix 1 contains the formal addresses made to the Robert Bosch Foundation Alumni Association at its annual conferences. Following the founding of the Alumni Association in New York in December 1985, it hosted two annual conferences in Washington, D.C. The first of these, in December 1986, invited Theo Sommer, editor in chief of *Die Zeit*, to address alumni and invited guests on the issue of Germany after the Reykjavik summit. His review of the summit and its implications for the 1987 elections was interesting and instructive. Horst Teltschik addressed the second annual conference in September 1987 on the German role in NATO and Europe, a timely and well-received presentation.

Due to the emphasis on professionals and career interests, the participants were selected for the Bosch program because of expertise in their respective fields. This is a strength of the Fellowship program and of the book. The authors all pursued careers in the United States in the same general field as the work performed at their guest institutions in the Federal Republic. The Fellows brought to their German colleagues several years of related experience in their field, and the benefit usually proved mutual. These varied experiences and backgrounds are applied here to a wide range of contemporary German issues.

The Robert Bosch Foundation Alumni Association

The objective of the Alumni Association in publishing this volume—*Germany Through American Eyes*—is to reinforce and further the purposes outlined in the association by-laws, which include:

- To provide a continuing education for former Bosch Fellows in current German and European social, political, and cultural issues

- To provide a forum for maintaining personal and professional contacts with German counterparts

- To create and foster contact and communication among successive groups of Bosch Fellows

- To encourage and foster any other such activity that has the purpose of promoting the long-term improvement of German-U.S. relations

The process of intensifying knowledge of Germany as well as exposure to the interests of U.S. colleagues continues today in the Alumni Association. The establishment of the Alumni Association has served the purpose of maintaining the high level of interest in Germany that the Fellows brought back to the United States. Many former Fellows participate in the regional alumni organizations that have been formed throughout the United States. Others participate in the various committees aimed at strengthening German-U.S. relations. Finally, each year there is an annual conference to bring the alumni together for discussions and debate with one another and with guest speakers. These conferences enable the alumni of the region in which it is held to identify the community interested in German affairs and to give impetus to future events dealing with German-U.S. issues.

Gale A. Mattox
John H. Vaughan, Jr.

Acknowledgments

This volume represents the efforts of a number of people. First and foremost, the Alumni Association owes a debt of gratitude to the Robert Bosch Foundation and its executive director, Peter Payer, as well as to the members of the Curatorium who generously agreed to fund the process by which the chapters were selected for publication. The chapters were submitted to the Robert Bosch Foundation from 1985 to 1987 as part of the Fellowship Program in which all the authors participated. Each of the chapters reflects the professional experiences of its author during the time spent as a Bosch Fellow in the Federal Republic of Germany. Robert Bosch Foundation Deputy Director Rüdiger Stephan also deserves a word of sincere thanks for his efforts in the publication of this volume.

The chapters were selected by a review board of outside experts. They included Werner Hein, Stephen Szabo, Karl Cerny, and Michael von Harper as well as alumni Joseph Blum, Geoffrey Oliver, John Schmitz, and Alex Kaplan. We thank them for their time and efforts.

The alumni were all supportive in a number of ways in our efforts to publish the chapters submitted to the Bosch Foundation at the conclusion of the program. We particularly thank the 1987–1988 Executive Board and its president, Brad Shingleton. Publication Committee members Karin Johnston and Constance Moran also deserve a special word of appreciation.

Finally, the lion's share of the work was done by the chapter authors, who provided updates and revisions, often under considerable time pressure. Their good nature and willingness to respond quickly made the entire process a rewarding experience for the editors.

G.A.M.
J.H.V., Jr.

The views expressed in the chapters are those of the authors and do not represent those of the institutions with which they are affiliated, the Robert Bosch Foundation, or the Robert Bosch Foundation Alumni Association.

Acronyms

AIF	Federation of Industrial Research Associations
BMFT	Bundesministerium für Forshung und Technologie
BMJ	Bundesministerium der Justiz
CDU	Christian Democratic Union
CPSU	Communist Party of the Soviet Union
CSCE	Conference on Security and Cooperation in Europe
CSU	Christian Social Union
DGB	Federal German Trade Union
DM	deutsche mark
FDP	Free Democratic Party
INF	intermediate-range nuclear forces
ICBM	intercontinental ballistic missile
MLF	Multilateral Force
MNE	multinational enterprise
OECD	Organization for Economic Cooperation and Development
SED	Socialist Unity Party
SPD	Social Democratic Party
VC	venture capital
VE	*Verrechnungseinheit*
WFG	Wagnisfinanzierung Gesellschaft
ZPO	Zivilprozessordnung

PART ONE

Foreign Policy Issues

1

Dilemmas of
an Atlantic Dialogue

Edwina S. Campbell

The year 1949 was a watershed year for foreign policy commitments and domestic repercussions for the United States and the Federal Republic of Germany (FRG). Since then, both have traveled a long road in the development of their national and international policies. Yet relations between the two countries have failed to reflect the sometimes divergent developments of nearly forty years. Their perceptions of, and wishful thinking about, each other have remained largely static.

West German–U.S. relations since the U.S. entrance into the North Atlantic Treaty Organization (NATO) and the establishment of the Federal Republic of Germany can be broken down into three phases. The first phase, 1949–1963, corresponded with the German chancellorship of Konrad Adenauer and with a U.S. focus on Western Europe that was historically atypical and logically unsustainable as well as undesirable much beyond the early 1960s.

The second phase, 1963–1975, was a period of transition within Europe and between the two sides of the Atlantic Alliance. This phase was characterized by an attempt to present these transitions as consistent with the previous fifteen years and to reconcile diverging U.S. and European interests rhetorically, if not substantially. Perhaps these attempts largely succeeded. Their legacy remains a key problem.

Finally, the third phase, 1975–1987, was filled with discontent and recrimination on both sides. The divergence of policies grew wider, and expectations for consultation and cooperation declined. Current West German–U.S. relations appear to be entering a fourth phase, one that will certainly not be pleasant, will likely be dangerous, and may potentially be destructive for both sides.

Phase One, 1949–1963

In the spring of 1949, the Truman administration completed negotiations for a Western security alliance with ten European countries and Canada, and the United States signed the North Atlantic Treaty. Shortly thereafter, the three Western powers (the United States, France, and Britain) agreed to the metamorphosis of their zones of occupation into the Federal Republic of Germany. Perhaps only a minority of those "present at the creation" of these two structures expected them to be playing a role in the international system at the end of the century. But an unexpected key event for U.S. and West German decisionmakers came a year later—the invasion of South Korea by North Korea in June 1950. The foreign policies of the United States and the FRG entered a period of frenetic diplomatic activity that was characterized by the common perception of a lack of options. The decisions set in motion in 1950 remained without serious domestic challenge in either country for the next fifteen years.

In the United States, the origin of the bipartisan consensus on foreign policy was clear. It represented the victory of those who had argued that the lack of a clear U.S. political and military commitment to the world order of the interwar years had encouraged and enabled the early victories of Italy, Japan, and Germany. Soviet actions in Europe had laid the basis for this group's ability to rally enough U.S. public and congressional opinion to support the North Atlantic Treaty. The war in Korea effectively silenced the opponents of any commitment in principle and those who had opposed a military (but not an economic) role for the United States outside the Americas.[1]

For Bonn, the U.S. reaction to the Korean conflict was the dominant event in the formation of West German foreign policy. The United States saw a need for increased conventional forces in Western Europe to reinforce NATO deterrence. In the fall of 1950, the United States called for the immediate creation of a West German army to contribute to the defense of Western Europe. This was a shift in U.S. foreign policy away from a supportive but secondary role for the FRG toward French attempts to integrate the FRG into the Schuman Plan's emerging European Coal and Steel Community. By moving farther and faster than Paris in demanding West German rearmament at a time when France was waging war in Indochina, Washington provoked two responses from the Fourth Republic: first, the Pleven Plan for the European Defense Community and second, ironically, the demand that U.S. (and British) troops be assigned to Europe in peacetime. The latter was precisely what the United States intended to prevent in the long term with the creation of the Bundeswehr (the German Armed Forces).[2]

In Bonn, U.S. insistence on West German rearmament established an enduring pattern of behavior. The FRG government developed a tendency to explain its foreign policy decisions to its constituents and, to a certain extent, to understand them itself as responses to demands made by the United States. Thus, in the 1950s, domestic opponents of rearmament and integration into NATO were labeled "anti-American" in a way that would simply have been unintelligible in other countries—including the United States. Decisions unpopular ten years after V-E Day were sold to public opinion as a way to restore (West) Germany's voice in the management of its own affairs and to thank the United States for Marshall Plan aid and the Berlin airlift. The U.S. connection achieved an importance that disquieted Paris and did a disservice to Washington; by 1963, both expected a positive knee-jerk reaction out of Bonn to policies initiated by the United States.

These expectations were largely justified until the mid-1960s. Given Adenauer's goal of restoring West German sovereignty, maintaining the economic miracle, and securing U.S. military guarantees, the Bonn-Washington axis was a useful instrumentality. But there were goals that could not be met by a Washington-focused policy, as Adenauer implicitly admitted with his 1955 trip to Moscow to secure the release of German POWs and his 1963 treaty with Charles de Gaulle's France to cement postwar Franco-German rapprochement. Moreover, the Washington focus was made possible by the narrowness of West German interests. In the Suez crisis of 1956, the 1958 U.S. landing in Lebanon, and the 1962 Cuban missile crisis, Bonn largely remained—as it was expected to be—silent. Expanding European political cooperation and West German economic and political interests had not yet made such silence untenable.

Phase Two, 1963–1975

By 1963, the postwar period was over. On both sides of the Atlantic, developing technologies combined with a new political environment to produce a climatic change in the alliance. The common wisdom was that, their economic recovery having succeeded, West Europeans would now share the burden of defense and deterrence with the United States in a NATO based on the "twin pillars" of Western Europe and North America. Symbolic of this were the 1960 reorganization of the Organization for European Economic Cooperation into the Organization for Economic Cooperation and Development (OECD), with U.S. membership, and the abortive Multilateral Force (MLF) proposal in NATO. Both the OECD and the MLF were attempts to reinforce the twin pillars concept of NATO. But the specific responses, like the twin pillars concept, were inadequate to achieve the true security partnership of Western Europe and the United States as envisioned by the concept.[3]

By 1963, the United States was vulnerable, as it had not been in 1949, to military attack on its own continental territory. The change in U.S. and, later, under U.S. pressure, NATO strategic doctrine from massive retaliation to flexible response reflected this U.S. vulnerability. But the implications of physical vulnerability went far deeper than was perceived at the time. The original U.S. commitment to Western Europe had rested on the two premises—that it was a short-term commitment, not requiring the stationing of U.S. troops abroad in peacetime, and that it posed no risk to, but was rather an enhancement of, the security of the United States.[4]

The first premise had already been undermined by the establishment of the Supreme Headquarters Allied Powers Europe under General Dwight Eisenhower in 1950, as a response to the war in Korea, and by the Western pledges given to France in exchange for West German rearmament. The second had been called into question even earlier by the Soviet Union's detonation of its atomic bomb in August 1949. But it was not until the development of Soviet intercontinental ballistic missiles (ICBMs) in the late 1950s that the risks of the U.S. commitment radically changed.

The contrasting U.S. reactions to the two major crises of the Kennedy administration brought home to many Europeans, not least of all to President de Gaulle, the uneven nature of the Atlantic Alliance. In October 1962, the United States went to the brink of war with the Soviet Union to prevent establishment of a Soviet missile base in Cuba. Fourteen months earlier, the same president had been unwilling to risk an all-out confrontation with the USSR over the erection of the wall dividing East and West Berlin. The three Western allies were content to assert their own rights in greater Berlin but not to insist on freedom of movement for Berliners, a lesson not lost on the city's governing mayor, Willy Brandt.[5]

In reality, the United States had always been unwilling to use either its nuclear arsenal or overt force in general to support its policies in Europe. This was clear as early as 1948 with the U.S. response to the Berlin blockade. The airlift was a compromise between retreat from Berlin and the forceable reopening of the land corridors to the Western sectors made possible by U.S. technological supremacy. The choice of the airlift occurred at a time when the United States had a monopoly on atomic power and overwhelming supremacy in the air for delivery of atomic and conventional systems. U.S. military policy had never been congruent with its rhetorical foreign policy of "rollback," but not until the 1961 Berlin crisis and the U.S. demand for a change in NATO's strategic doctrine was this made patently clear to the Europeans.[6]

The doctrine of flexible response was only one sign, however, of the changing relationship between Moscow and Washington. The establishment of the Agency for International Development and the Green Berets reflected growing U.S. concern for areas of the world outside Europe, where developments could not be effectively influenced by threats of massive retaliation on Moscow. Even without Soviet ICBMs, the foreign policies of Peking, Havana, and New Delhi would have compelled the United States to seek new responses in areas of the globe where both superpowers were beginning to find that their control was elusive.

On the surface, this situation set up a short-term congruity of interests among the United States, the USSR, and Western Europe. But while the superpowers sought to manage their rivalry in a world grown more volatile technologically and politically, Western Europe was faced increasingly with a situation in which negotiation and compromise with Moscow, not alliance with Washington, offered the only path to achievement of foreign policy goals. This situation was particularly acute for the West Germans. As embodied in the Hallstein Doctrine, which mandated a cessation of relations with any states recognizing East Germany, Bonn's foreign policy toward Eastern Europe was neither credible nor sustainable in an increasingly multipolar world.[7]

In the 1960s, however, the long-term implication of these diverging U.S. and European goals was far from apparent. Essentially content with the postwar order, the United States and the USSR sought to manage it in a changing world. Essentially discontent with this order, the West Germans began their efforts to transform it without the use of force and, after 1968, without attempting to bypass Moscow. Two events at the time disguised the extent of the differences between Bonn and Washington—France's withdrawal from the NATO integrated military structure in 1966 and the Warsaw Pact invasion of Czechoslovakia in 1968. Faced almost simultaneously with these two crises, neither capital was prepared to wager its ties with the other. Within NATO, the 1967 *Harmel Report on the Future Tasks of the Alliance* successfully attempted to bring together the various viewpoints of fifteen allies. It added to the two earlier tasks of defense and deterrence a third: détente, which was defined as negotiations between the two blocs to achieve "a more stable relationship in which the underlying political issues can be solved."[8] With the Harmel Report, the Grand Coalition of the Christian Democratic Union (CDU) and the Social Democratic Party (SPD) achieved a priori alliance approval of what became the *Ost-* and *Deutschlandpolitik* of the next government.

But the success of the Harmel exercise was deceptive. Its dichotomies were best typified by the 1971 Quadripartite Agreement on Berlin, which reaffirmed the de facto status quo of 1945 and, in the short run, opened the way for conclusion of the Basic Treaty between the two German states. In the long run, however, the agreement meant something quite different to Moscow and Washington than it did to Bonn. For the superpowers, it was the *closing* of an era of disputes and discussions about their respective roles in Berlin. For the West Germans, it was the *opening* of a process that was designed in the long run to overhaul the postwar status quo, including that part of it reaffirmed by the Quadripartite Agreement.

Like the Quadripartite Agreement, the 1975 Final Act of the Conference on Security and Cooperation in Europe (CSCE) was much more the end of an era for Moscow and Washington than it was for Bonn. The Helsinki follow-up conferences offered opportunities to the FRG that were, to the two superpowers, at best superfluous and at worst destabilizing in terms of their influence within their respective blocs. Nevertheless, this difference in perspective between Washington and Bonn remained unarticulated until the breakdown of the East-West détente process in the late 1970s. Eventually, West German and U.S. disagreements about the future of détente brought into focus the question of whether the U.S. connection and the structures established to maintain it had become a hindrance to the pursuit of West German foreign policy goals.

Phase Three, 1975–1987

One of the great failures of U.S. foreign policy since 1969 has been its inability to analyze correctly the original domestic consensus created by Willy Brandt in support of Bonn's *Ostpolitik*[9] and the evolution of that consensus under Chancellors Helmut Schmidt and Helmut Kohl. In 1969, after three years as foreign minister, Brandt entered the chancellory with the support of a broad spectrum of public opinion in favor of initiatives to normalize West German relations with Eastern Europe. He was reelected in 1972 with an even broader consensus in support of his *Ostpolitik* and its global implications including membership of the two German states in the United Nations and a broader field of action for West German foreign policy in the Third World.

The breadth of this political spectrum made possible the chancellor's initiatives, but it also made vulnerable the delicate balance between West German Atlanticism and West Germany's relations with the East. The consensus was inherently volatile, encompassing convinced Atlanticists, who were in fact ready to jettison the *Ostpolitik* if it threatened relations with Washington, and young and old Social Democrats, who saw the *Ostpolitik* as a first step to achievement of their pre-Godesberg foreign policy goals—demilitarization of central Europe and reunification of Germany through a process of disengagement of the wartime allies.[10]

By the time Helmut Schmidt became chancellor in 1974, it was apparent that these goals were not going to be achieved in the short run. The resulting disillusionment contributed to the fracturing of the SPD's left wing and the establishment of the Greens and the Alternatives, with a clearly defined, bloc-free foreign policy program. Brandt had had to signify many things to many people to create his original consensus; Schmidt's dilemma was to prevent the *Westpolitik*,[11] and specifically the Bonn-Washington axis, from being seen as, and from becoming, an obstacle to the process opened in the preceding five years. He got little help from the United States.

Neither President Jimmy Carter nor his Republican successor understood that the NATO dual-track decision in December 1979 was a political necessity for Schmidt and his party, without which the SPD would not have survived the 1980 election intact. The dual-track decision called for arms control negotiations with the East immediately and, in 1983, the deployment of intermediate-range nuclear forces (or INF—in this case, 572 ground-launched cruise missiles and Pershing IIs) in Western Europe, if the negotiations had not successfully removed the Soviet INF threat. Within the party, the Brandt coalition had collapsed, with the former chancellor the most prominent critic of policies too oriented to those of Washington. The structure of the SPD, with leadership divided between its chair and its chancellor, and the structure of the coalition, with foreign policy enunciated by its Social Democratic chancellor and its Free Democratic foreign minister, should have signaled Washington that its Atlanticist assumptions had become dangerously outdated, but such was not the case.

Preoccupied with crises in Iran, Afghanistan, and Nicaragua, the Carter administration pursued an erratic foreign policy course that culminated in the unilateral and precipitous abandonment of dialogue with the Soviet Union in late 1979, the failed rescue attempt of the U.S. hostages in Iran (contradicting U.S. pledges of nonuse of force in exchange for European economic sanctions), and the boycott of the 1980 Moscow Olympics. Only the dual-track decision and the U.S. pledge to observe the unratified Strategic Arms Limitation Talks (SALT) II agreement gave Chancellor Schmidt a basis on which to balance the factions of his party and his coalition.[12]

Ronald Reagan's 1980 electoral victory and his appointment of a former Supreme Allied Commander of Europe, General Al Haig, as secretary of state initially raised West German hopes of a new continuity in U.S. foreign policy. The opposition of President Reagan to SALT II was worrisome, but two Republican administrations had been the SPD's partners in détente. Washington's failure to understand the erosion of Atlanticism in West Germany was, however, more than matched by Bonn's failure to understand the same development in the United States. Support for the alliance in the United States, despite the rhetoric of its early constituency, was historically even more fragile than it was in the FRG.

The Reagan victory represented a clear rejection of the policies of his immediate predecessor; but it was also a rejection of the link between an activist U.S. foreign policy and the Atlantic Alliance. To the previous options of isolationism and internationalism, the new administration added a third option—unilateral internationalism. According to this option, the United States could pursue its security interests more effectively if not constrained to arrive at a policy of the least common denominator with its European allies. The articulation of this foreign policy during the first eighteen months of the Reagan administration did not alone bring down the SPD-led coalition in Bonn, but it made the chancellor's balancing act within his party impossible, to the point where a battle-scarred SPD went disarrayed, but almost palpably relieved, into opposition in 1982.[13]

Washington's hopes for a return to the good old days of the first CDU chancellor were ill-founded from the start. The assumption that the new CDU government, or any conceivable West German government, would automatically line up with Washington on issues such as the Soviet-European gas pipeline, was wildly out of focus with reality. The new CDU/Free Democratic Party (FDP) government was inevitably to confront the same stresses in its relations with Washington as had its predecessor. Given the foreign policy perspective of the U.S. administration, the task of managing these stresses was to become more, not less, difficult, despite the chancellor's apparent predisposition to get along personally with the president.[14]

Moreover, the old instincts remained. Finding that the substance of its foreign policy goals was often not compatible with that of Washington, Bonn reacted in ways already well developed in the first two phases of U.S.–West German relations. From the first phase remained the familiar pattern of explaining decisions to the West German electorate as responses to demands by the U.S. ally. The path of least resistance precluded a domestic political debate on West German interests by asserting that the government had no choice but to go along with the United States. This strategy degenerated into a tendency to portray the United States as an ally in need of constraint and to claim that only West German acceptance of a particular policy offered the possibility of exerting a restraining influence. Bonn's reaction to the U.S. proposal for the Strategic

Defense Initiative in the period 1983–1986 was an almost textbook example of this tendency.

The CDU-led coalition retained its predecessors' proclivity for papering over the fundamental cleavage in the West German foreign policy consensus. The Atlantic consensus was gone, but the tendency to say comforting things to the United States about the Washington-Bonn axis was so ingrained that few West German policymakers could even see the problem, much less deal with it. The reality of diverging aims and means emerged, not in the rhetoric employed with the United States, but in the policies pursued in areas not directly related to NATO. But whether in Europe or in the Third World, attempts to find a new gravitational pole for Bonn's foreign policy, around which West German interests could be independently defined, were endangered by the common tendency of the SPD's left wing and the CDU's right wing to react to Washington, rather than to assess a policy's advantages to the FRG.

Phase Four: Prospects for the Future

Underlying the tensions and the dissembling on both sides of the Atlantic is a fundamental difference in attitude toward the postwar status quo. The United States can conceive of a better order in central Europe—open borders, freer communication, and economic growth—but it can also conceive of a worse one. The strict division between East and West is not the first U.S. preference, but it is more congenial than many other possibilities. Running the risk of confrontation with the Soviet Union by supporting change in the status quo is something the United States, except at a rhetorical level, has never been willing to do. But, on a less conscious level, Washington, not unlike Paris, is perfectly comfortable with the situation as it is. The FRG is a congenially-sized German state and an economic asset to the West. The proclivity to avoid destabilizing changes, even through negotiations, is something that unites Paris, Washington, and Moscow. But not Bonn. The organizational inertia that also causes both superpowers to cling to the structures they know—Warsaw Pact or NATO—is not unknown in the FRG, but the West Germans have strong countervailing interests that decrease the influence of this inertia.

The crucial development of the third phase was not the neutralist nationalism of the German Left, which attracted so much attention in Washington and Paris. Rather, the crucial development, which went unnoticed by successive U.S. administrations was Bonn's definition of common interests and its establishment of a network of ties with the governments of Warsaw Pact countries, including East Berlin.[15] This network is spreading outward and downward, paralleling the growth of immediate postwar relations with France, to include educational exchange and sister cities programs. The network is still lopsided, in terms of the money, time, and effort the FRG, its states, and its communities give to cultivate these ties. But to the West German government and people, this is nothing new; for better or worse, such was the pattern of postwar relations with France and the United States as well.

Unobserved by its U.S. ally, West Germany has found its natural allies in the governments and peoples of Eastern Europe, while attempting to restructure the postwar status quo. The attempt is not uncontroversial. The reluctance of Willy Brandt to meet with Solidarity leader Lech Wałęsa while on a visit to Poland is disquieting to the SPD, which is elsewhere in the world a rhetorical champion of human rights. The question of defining German borders in the East reemerges to trouble the CDU, as Germans from the East face old age and death with no prospect of returning to their birthplaces. Commercial interests sometimes seem to be of overriding concern in an export-oriented West Germany struggling to push down the unemployment rate and searching for new markets.

But the debates about how, how far, and how fast to restructure its relations with the East are tactical. They disguise the fact that along the West German political spectrum, the debate about whether to pursue such policies no longer exists. At CSCE follow-up forums in Budapest and Bern, at the Mutual and Balanced Force Reduction talks in Vienna, and during bilateral visits to Albania, Yugoslavia, and the Warsaw Pact countries, West German officials have succeeded in countering the German historical image with a new image of the FRG as a reliable partner in overcoming the division of Europe. Eastern Europe also has a successor generation, unfettered by personal memories of war and occupation, that is searching for a magnet in the West. But the postwar elites of these countries have no interest in destablizing the systems that brought them their own status. Links between the East and the FRG promise change and stability in a way that ties with the United States would not. One of Bonn's assets is the history of German linguistic and cultural dominance in Eastern and Central Europe, now that the political overtones of this dominance are receding.[16]

Remarkably, West German politicians have so far succeeded in carrying out the pragmatic, but doomed, policies of Weimar foreign minister Gustav Stresemann. His attempt to "hollow out" the restrictions of Versailles floundered in the late 1920s on the world economic situation, criticism from the radical Right and Left, and the inability of the German negotiating partners to trust Berlin enough. Bonn's attempts to hollow out the rigidities of the post-1945 European order have so far been carried out with a patience and, since the 1970s, with a domestic consensus that Stresemann could only envy. But the same pitfalls lie on the road ahead. The willingness of the Christian Democratic Party to face the wrath of its own far Right and cease encouraging illusions of a new German political dominance in Eastern Europe and of the SPD to face the wrath of its own far Left and to cease encouraging illusions of an apolitical Central Europe that simply opts out of the international system will be crucial. So will the policies of Moscow and of Bonn's allies in the West.

With the arrival of Mikhail Gorbachev in the Kremlin, new possibilities for changes in the European status quo opened for the FRG. Bonn's interest in the nature of the borders between the states of Europe, East and West (not in the existence of those borders per se) reflects a mixture of supranational economic-political integration and the Gaullist concept of interstate cooperation that has developed in Western Europe during the past quarter century. The essential element of the West European model is the free movement of goods, people, and ideas, which is well on its way to achievement.

Looking eastward, Bonn confronts the clear interest the peoples of Eastern Europe have long had in achieving the same goal. Since 1985, Bonn also confronts a Soviet leader who seems to understand that his country's self-interest demands a level of exchange with the West unprecedented in its history. The April 1986 accident at Chernobyl dramatically underscored this, and West German foreign policy responded by emphasizing that technological cooperation also required a willingness to expand "human contacts" in the "common European house."[17] In 1987, these contacts on the inner-German level reached an unprecedented level: Nearly 20 percent of the population of the German Democratic Republic—more than 3 million people, including 1.2 million nonpensioners—visited West Germany.[18] The prospects for Bonn's foreign policy in the 1990s hinge on the success of Gorbachev's reforms at home and on his ability to find allies within the new generation of Warsaw Pact leadership that will emerge.

These prospects also hinge on the ability of the United States to reemphasize the original goals of its postwar policy toward Europe— political stability, economic prosperity, and military security. As the principal partner in an alliance created to achieve the stability and security of Western Europe, Washington shaped the *Westpolitik* that made the early initiatives of the *Ostpolitik* possible. But clinging to a structure designed to deal with a particular historical moment—the war-weary Western Europe of the Stalin years—and to a status quo that is eminently unsatisfactory to the key European member of the alliance in the long run can only be counterproductive to U.S. foreign policy. There is no long-term U.S. interest served by clinging to 1945, as the French once did to 1919.

Moreover, the success of the European Community and the emergence of new centers of power in other parts of the world encourage the United States to turn its attention to U.S. interests outside Europe. Indeed, this shift marks a return to the normal worldview of U.S. foreign policy, to which the Eurocentric years 1945–1960 were the exception. That these interests may demand unilateral action that will not command the support of West Europeans, and vice versa, needs to be recognized by both sides. To ignore such differences will be fatal in the long run. Misguided attempts to save the alliance will destroy the Atlantic relationship.

One of the principal differences between Washington and Bonn is the extent to which their interests are served by the postwar European status quo. The advantages that appear obvious on the Potomac seem quite the opposite on the Rhine. The risks to be run in changing that status quo seem worth it along Bonn's Adenauerallee in a way that is not easily explained in Washington's Foggy Bottom. Thirty years ago, a Canadian architect of NATO called on Canada's allies to engage in frank talk with each other, to make their dialogue "a mixture between a confessional and a Quaker meeting."[19] Unfortunately, the Bonn-Washington dialogue has come very close to being a dialogue of the deaf. Avoiding that fate in the years to come will require more candor than the two countries have recently been able to muster, but the sound of two voices arguing will serve them better than the sound of silence.

Notes

1. Robert R. Bowie, "Die Zusammenarbeit der politischen Fuehrungsgruppen," *Amerika und Westeuropa: Gegenwarts- und Zukunftsprobleme*, ed. Karl Kaiser and Hans-Peter Schwarz (Stuttgart: Belser Verlag, 1977), pp. 46–49, is an interesting discussion of early Atlantic cooperation.

2. See Alfred Grosser, *Affaires Exterieures* (Paris: Flammarion, 1984), pp. 79–89, on the Schuman and Pleven Plans.

3. See Henry A. Kissinger, *The Troubled Partnership* (New York: McGraw Hill, 1965).

4. Timothy Ireland, *Creating the Entangling Alliance* (Westport, Conn.: Greenwood, 1980), is the best treatment of adding NATO's "O."

5. Willy Brandt, *Begegnungen und Einsichten* (Hamburg: Hoffmann und Campe, 1976), pp. 9–41.

6. The significance of the Berlin Wall for U.S.–West German relations has been well analyzed by David Gress, notably in his *Peace and Survival* (Stanford, Calif.: Hoover Institution, 1985), pp. 23–45.

7. See, for example, Willy Brandt's discussion of his years as foreign minister, *Begegnungen*, pp. 185–218.

8. *NATO Final Communiques, 1949–74* (Brussels: NATO Information Service, n.d.), p. 198.

9. *Ostpolitik* is the term given to an aspect of West German foreign policy that was begun in the late 1960s at the instigation of the SPD and was designed to broaden contacts and reduce tensions with the Soviet Union and Communist Eastern Europe.

10. See Lewis Edinger, *Kurt Schumacher* (London: Oxford University Press, 1965), pp. 144–189, on the SPD's foreign policy before 1959.

11. *Westpolitik* is a term used by the FRG to describe its relations with fellow member states in NATO and the European Community.

12. Helmut Schmidt's comment that Germany "will not be bound to the West by an American president coming from Georgia, California, or any other state; [but only] by the West Europeans," in his *A Grand Strategy for the West* (New Haven, Conn.: Yale University Press, 1985), p. 56, reflected the tenor of his last years in office.

13. The preceding two paragraphs are based on discussions with senior political and government officials in Bonn, 1985–1986.

14. Richard Loewenthal, "The German Question Transformed," *Foreign Affairs* (Winter 1984-85), pp. 303–315, analyzed the bipartisan consensus on *Ostpolitik* that has developed in Bonn since 1972.

15. A good overview of these years can be found in the contributions to *Zwanzig Jahre Ostpolitik*, ed. Horst Ehmke, Karlheinz Koppe, and Herbert Wehner (Bonn: Neue Gesellschaft, 1986).

16. Discussions with West German and other senior officials in Bonn, West Berlin, Stockholm, and Vienna, 1985–1986.

17. The best statement of this approach is Foreign Minister Hans-Dietrich Genscher's speech to the Danube-European Institute in Vienna, August 27, 1986, "Perspektiven einer europaischen Friedensordnung," *Bulletin* 96 (August 29, 1986), pp. 807–813.

18. This is nearly twenty-four times the number of East German nonpensioners who visited in 1985; see *Deutschland-Nachrichten* (New York: German Information Service, January 6, 1988), p. 3.

19. Lester Pearson in *Mike: The Memoirs of the Right Honorable Lester B. Pearson*, ed. John A. Munro and Alex I. Inglis (New York: Quadrangle, 1973), pp. 2, 65.

2

Formal Recognition as a Means of Advancing *Deutschlandpolitik*

Kathryn S. Mack

The official position of the government of the Federal Republic of Germany (FRG) is that two German states, but only one German nation, exist. The German Democratic Republic (GDR) is not considered a foreign country, and international law is not thought to govern the content of the relationship between the two states. The West German government is bound to this legal theory by a 1973 Federal Constitutional Court judgment[1] that upheld the constitutionality of the Treaty on the Basis of Intra-German Relations Between the FRG and the GDR (the Basic Treaty). In this judgment, the court reasoned that because the preamble and Articles 16, 23, 116 and 146 of the Basic Law[2] assume that the German Reich still exists as a legal entity, although without state organs, the GDR cannot be seen as a foreign state but must be considered as part of the German Reich. This interpretation of the Basic Law places a constitutional barrier in the way of future West German formal recognition of the GDR. In addition, pursuant to Section 31 of the Statute on the Constitutional Court, the court's judgment is given the force of statute. Although usually only the tenor of a decision has binding effect, the court in this particular case purposely stated that the rationale as well was to be binding.[3] In this manner, the court has legislated future government policy: State organs are prevented from formally recognizing the GDR.

Although these major constitutional and statutory impediments make the issue of formal recognition moot for the present, the purpose of this chapter is to begin the discussion on the possible benefits West Germany could derive by compromising on this issue. Under the current legal framework, West Germany is at the same time able to acknowledge the four-power control over Berlin and to treat West Berlin as part of the

17

FRG for purposes of inter-German trade and citizenship. Only if recognition of the GDR preserved and strengthened these and other ties between West Berlin and the FRG would a change in the status quo be of interest to the West German government. This chapter will argue in favor of an exchange in which West Germany would recognize the GDR in return for the GDR and the Soviet Union acknowledging the close relationship that exists between West Berlin and the FRG. After an examination of the legal underpinnings of the one-nation theory that defines the status quo, the necessary requirements the Soviet Union and East Germany would have to meet in order to induce West Germany to recognize East Germany will be analyzed and the effect of recognition on the special relationship between the two countries will be reviewed.

The One-Nation Theory

Two different, conflicting legal theories exist to explain the one-nation theory advocated by West Germany: the *Identitätstheorie* (theory of identity) and the *Dachtheorie* (roof theory).[4] As the original theory advanced by Bonn, the *Identitätstheorie* provides that the FRG is identical with the still existing German Reich. In the past, this theory allowed West Germany (1) to assert that it was the only legitimate representative for the whole of Germany in foreign affairs and (2) to refuse to establish or maintain diplomatic relations with any state that established full diplomatic relations with the GDR. As GDR power increased, however, the FRG had increasing difficulty applying this theory consistently.[5]

Beginning with Willy Brandt's *Ostpolitik*, a new legal theory, the *Dachtheorie*, was espoused that held the two parts of Germany were two German communities connected under the common roof formed by the still existent German Reich.[6] The *Dachtheorie* allowed Brandt to accept the existence of two equal German states and permit all other third countries to recognize the GDR under international law and, at the same time, to maintain that neither Germany could be considered a foreign state to the other. According to the West German government, a special relationship governed by domestic law (*Staatsrecht*) exists between the German states somewhat similar to the relationship among the states of the British Commonwealth.[7]

In determining the constitutionality of the Basic Treaty, the Federal Constitutional Court, unwilling to choose between the two legal theories, reaffirmed both. Therefore, West Germany is simultaneously identical and partly identical with the German Reich.[8] Furthermore, by attempting to force upon the GDR a special relationship that it unequivocally denies, both the *Identitätstheorie* and the *Dachtheorie* conflict with Bonn's promise in the Basic Treaty to respect GDR independence, sovereign jurisdiction, and autonomy in external and internal affairs.

The Federal Constitutional Court in its judgment attempted to give substance to the one-nation theory by emphasizing the unique practical aspects of the relationshp between the two Germanys that the Basic Treaty maintained. The most important of these were:

- the four-power control over Germany as a whole

- the establishment by West Germany of a "mission" in East Berlin rather than a diplomatic embassy

- the inter-German system of trade

- the homogenous German citizenship based on the Reich's law of 1913

Only the four-power control over Germany as a whole and Berlin in particular represents a situation under international law in which the relationship between the two Germanys is not one between two fully sovereign powers. Although the establishment of a "mission" in East Berlin, the inter-German system of trade, and the German citizenship statute all emphasize the peculiar relationship between the two countries, the peculiarity arises from the West German approach to the situation rather than from international law.

The legal underpinnings of the West German one-nation theory are thus both inconsistent and amorphous in nature. Nonetheless, as a result of the 1973 judgment by the Federal Constitutional Court, any attempt by Bonn to use the one-nation theory as a bargaining chip in its relations with East Germany would require an amendment to the Basic Law. Such an amendment requires a two-thirds majority of the Bundestag. As a result, the legal course between the two Germanys is not chartered for substantial change in the near future. At such time, however, as Bonn is able to convince the Bundestag that important advantages can be won by compromising on the issue of recognition, a new legal theory more consistent with the factual realities can be adopted.

Preconditions to Recognition

Berlin, which represents the point of collision between the Western and Eastern legal theories, has long been the focus of great political tension. Disagreement exists between the East and the West on two major legal issues: the four-power control over Greater Berlin[9] and the nature of the ties between the FRG and West Berlin. According to the

West, the four-power control applies to Greater Berlin as a whole, and the FRG and West Berlin have close political, economic, and cultural ties. In contrast, the East argues that only the Western sectors of the city remain a special political entity under military occupation; East Berlin has become an integral part of the GDR;[10] and West Berlin has no special relationship with the FRG. The Quadripartite Agreement, signed by the four allied powers on September 3, 1971, attempted to minimize these tensions by using ambiguous language to obscure the different legal interpretations underlying the agreement so as to arrive at concrete improvements in transportation ties between the FRG and West Berlin and in visitation rights from West Berlin to the GDR. Before West Germany could recognize East Germany, however, the four-power occupation status over Greater Berlin, to the extent such occupation status is acknowledged by the East under the Quadripartite Agreement, would have to be reaffirmed and the nature of the relationship between the Western sectors of the city and the FRG redefined.

The legal position of the Western powers is based on the "London Protocol of September 12, 1944 on the Zones of Occupation in Germany and the Administration of Greater Berlin," as amended, among Great Britain, the Soviet Union, the United States, and France, which divided Germany and Berlin into four sectors. In Berlin, supreme authority was exercised jointly by the Inter-Allied Governing Authority for Berlin (the Kommandatura) rather than by the individual military governors of each of the four sectors. In the summer of 1948, this system ended when the Soviets announced that they would no longer participate in any staff meetings of the Kommandatura. The Kommandatura has since worked on a tripartite basis in the Western sector with the Soviets participating only in the Air Safety Center.

Because the four-power status of the London protocols applied to all Berlin, the Western powers argue that the Soviet Union cannot unilaterally terminate such agreements. According to the Western powers, the Soviet Union may pull out of the Kommandatura and grant the GDR increasing rights in the eastern part of Berlin, but such actions cannot undercut the four-power status of the entire city under international law.[11] If recognition were to interfere with the occupation status of Berlin, it would not be permitted by the Western powers[12] and would not be desired by the West Germans because of the threat it would pose to the security of the city. Recognition of the GDR, however, would not have any negative effect on the four-power status of the city. Any new agreement among the four powers could follow the precedent established in the Quadripartite Agreement, in which the four powers reaffirmed their existing rights in the "relevant area."[13] Whereas for the three Western allies this term covered all of Berlin, for the Soviets it covered only the western sectors. Although there would be no meeting of the minds on the issue of whether East Berlin remained under four-power control, each side could continue to uphold its legal position.

Although ambiguity could be allowed to govern the four-power status issue, there must be a clear meeting of the minds among the four powers and the two Germanys on the issue of ties between West Berlin and the FRG. The various players involved can be divided into three groups: the West Germans; the Western powers; and the GDR and the Soviet Union. According to the East Germans and the Soviets, West Berlin is "an autonomous (special) political entity" on the territory of East Germany and has no right to any political ties with the FRG. The Western powers' view is that although close ties exist between West Berlin and the FRG, West Berlin is not a *Land* (state) of the FRG under international law.

Because Berlin is an island surrounded by an area under control of GDR authorities backed by Soviet forces, the Western allies have been very cautious to uphold their rights in Berlin by avoiding too close an association of the FRG with the operation of the Western sectors. For this reason, the allies suspended application to West Berlin of Article 23 of the Basic Law, which declared Greater Berlin to be a *Land* of the FRG. On the other hand, the Western allies permit the integration of the Western sectors in the economic, legal, financial, and customs system of the FRG. For the most part, every law and ordinance adopted by the FRG is applied to West Berlin as long as the allies, which have final decision in all matters of status and security, have no reservations. The inclusion of West Berlin in the international treaties and undertakings of the FRG is permitted unless objections are raised by the Western allies. In addition, West Berlin maintains a consultative status in the Bundestag and Bundesrat.

The legal position of the FRG differs from that of the allies only to the extent that Berlin is considered a *Land* of the FRG. Although the application of the Basic Law is limited on certain issues as a result of the occupation provisions, the validity of the law is maintained. As a result, the West Germans refer to the city as a *Land,* when dealing with West Berlin as a domestic issue, but when dealing with West Berlin in the international arena or in talks with the GDR, refer to it as a separate entity.

In Part IIB of the Quadripartite Agreement, the four powers agreed that "the ties between the Western Sectors of Berlin and the FRG will be maintained and developed, taking into account that these sectors continue not to be a constituent part of the FRG and not to be governed by it." In the past, great controversy has surrounded the interpretation of this section of the treaty, with both the East and the West emphasizing the words that support their respective theory.[14] The GDR and the Soviet

Union emphasize the terms of limitation in an attempt to define the ties between the FRG and West Berlin as no different from those that West Berlin could establish with any third state. West Germany and the Western powers emphasize that the agreement assumes the status quo and provides that such ties between the two may actually develop. Furthermore, the West argues that the ties are nowhere limited to economic, legal, or collateral spheres; they may also include political connections.

The majority of attempts by Bonn to develop ties with West Berlin have resulted in strong reactions from the Eastern bloc. Although as a result of such strong reactions the West has exercised increasing restraint, the East has not reciprocated by reducing its protests. A major West German compromise on the question of recognition could only be forthcoming if the East Germans and Soviets offered in return a compromise on the issue of West Berlin. First, the Soviet Union would have to be willing to agree with the other three powers to increase the ties between West Berlin and the FRG to the greatest extent possible without actually making the city a *Land* of the FRG, and second, East Germany would have to agree for all practical purposes to treat the Western sectors of the city as part of the FRG.

In particular, West Berlin would have to be treated as part of West Germany for purposes of inter-German trade, and FRG representation of West Berlin in the international arena would have to be accepted. Agreement would also have to be reached among the four powers to treat the residents of West Berlin as West German citizens. Despite the ratification of the FRG Basic Law in 1949, West German citizenship continues to be controlled by the Reichs- und Staatsangehörigkeitsgesetz of July 22, 1913,[15] that grants German nationality to all people living within the borders of the German Reich as of 1937. No new citizenship particular to the FRG has ever been adopted.[16] The 1913 law keeps the concept of a homogenous German people alive; despite the territorial division, in theory all East Germans and residents of Berlin have the same "German" citizenship rights as West Germans.[17] Any new West German statute regulating citizenship would therefore have to include the residents of West Berlin as citizens of the FRG.

If such compromises were made by the Eastern bloc and West Germany in turn granted formal recognition to East Germany, the relations between the two Germanys could be substantially normalized. Recognition of the GDR would not terminate the special links that bind the two countries, but rather would strengthen such links by further depoliticizing the relationship.

The Continuation of a Special Relationship

If the GDR were recognized by the FRG, the special relationship between the two states would continue under international law and in practice. Under international law, as already mentioned, the four-power status of Berlin and Germany as a whole would remain unchanged until the four powers negotiated a new treaty establishing a different framework for postwar Germany. In practice, West Germany's sense of moral responsibility to the East German people would also continue. The strength of this feeling was demonstrated in 1983 when West Germany was the only country willing to extend a loan to the GDR at a time when the latter's total debt to the West was approximately $12.5 billion and it was unable to meet debt-service payments from current income. In order to encourage the hesitant West German banks to enter into the transaction, the West German government intervened by agreeing to guarantee the loans. Such financial intermediation by the West German government is rare, particularly when the funds are not tied to the purchase of West German exports.[18] Although by tinkering with the market for political reasons the West German government was potentially opening itself up to criticism, a strong domestic consensus supported the action.

In addition, West Germany would continue to work closely with the GDR on a number of issues, including the improvement of transportation ties and conditions in the western sector of the city in exchange for monetary payments to East Berlin[19] and emigration and travel opportunities for East Germans to West Germany. Beginning in 1962, the West German government initiated a program to purchase the freedom of political prisoners in the GDR; an estimated 60,000 prisoners were "purchased" between 1962 and 1984 at an estimated cost of DM 1 billion.[20]

Recognition of East Germany, however, poses two possible threats to inter-German trade: first, that such trade would come under the control of the European Community (EC), and second, that East Germany would no longer wish to maintain a special trade relationship with West Germany. Given that economic exchanges between the two Germanys constitute one of the most important aspects of *Deutschlandpolitik*,[21] it is crucial to West Germany that such trade be allowed to continue. Trade between the two states is seen by the West German government as a means of improving the daily lives of the East German people, of preventing the GDR from integrating too rapidly into the Eastern bloc, of maintaining access to West Berlin, and of linking the two states together.[22]

In 1957, to encourage West Germany to join the EC, the other EC members agreed to amend the Treaty Establishing the European Economic Community (the EC Treaty)[23] so as to define inter-German trade as domestic trade, thereby giving West Germany unilateral control over its relations with East Germany. Other community members, in contrast, trade with East Germany as if dealing with a third state outside the community. The preamble to the Protocol amending the EC Treaty emphasized that this exception for West Germany arose out of "the conditions at present existing" by reason of the division of Germany.[24] Nowhere in the Protocol or the EC Treaty, however, was this phrase defined.

At first glance, it would appear that once the GDR is recognized, trade could no longer be labeled domestic, which would make the exception provided by the Protocol inapplicable. The reality, as history shows, is more complex. In 1972, the Basic Treaty was signed by the two Germanys establishing a new relationship between the two states based on equality and sovereignty in their foreign and domestic relations. Despite the increased international status of the GDR, both Germanys agreed in the Supplementary Protocol of the Basic Treaty that trade between them should "continue to be developed on the basis of existing agreements."[25] The agreements to which they were referring were the Interzonal Trade Agreement, otherwise known as the Berlin Agreement, which regulated inter-German trade, and the Protocol.

The other EC members were not obligated to uphold the decision of the Federal Constitutional Court that the Basic Treaty reaffirmed the inter-se relationship between the two German states. Indeed, each of the EC members at that time recognized two sovereign German states. The Protocol's definition of inter-German trade as trade between different parts of one German nation had become for them a legal fiction.[26] Nonetheless, the EC member states and community institutions raised no challenges to the continued applicability of the Protocol to the inter-German trade system.[27] The status quo was maintained despite the major change in GDR status because for West Germany the issue of inter-German trade remained as important as it had been in the past and because the EC members were willing to continue supporting that interest.

The West German abandonment of the one-nation theory would not represent a lessening of Bonn's interest in the whole of Germany, in the human rights of the Germans living in the East, or in the eventual reunification of the two countries. Indeed, as in 1973, maintenance of the special trade system would remain a priority for Bonn. Although the inter-German trade would no longer have to be defined as "domestic" trade, the EC members could amend the Protocol to grant West Germany continued unilateral control over inter-German trade based on the continuation of a special relationship between the two states. In all likelihood, EC members would once again support Bonn's interest as a matter of comity because of the West German economic importance in the EC as a net contributor of funds and because of the low economic cost of such a policy to them.

Assuming that the EC member states permit West Germany to continue regulating its own trade relations with the GDR, the second question is whether the GDR would be interested in continuing a special trade relationship with West Germany. Established in 1951 by the Berlin Agreement, the inter-German trade system was designed to facilitate trade and to support the West German one-nation theory. By defining the area effected by the agreement in terms of the two currency areas, deutsche mark west and deutsche mark east, the Berlin Agreement treated West Berlin as part of the FRG and officially avoided recognizing the GDR.

Even though East Germany would be free to enter into new trade agreements, in all likelihood it would continue employing a system similar to that established under the Berlin Agreement because of the substantial economic benefits it receives. The basic manner in which inter-German trade operates is that the two central banks (the Bundesbank and the GDR Staatsbank, previously Deutsche Notenbank) are responsible for operating a clearing arrangement whereby each credits imports to and debits exports from the other's currency area to an account of the other's central bank. The bilateral clearing trade is based on the DM west, but payment is made in a clearing unit of account (the *Verrechnungseinheit,* or VE).

The three primary advantages of this system of trade for the GDR are an interest-free overdraft referred to as the swing; an exemption from import duties normally imposed on non-EC third-country goods; and tax incentives that permit West German importers to deduct 11 percent of the value of their GDR imports from their turnover taxes. Aside from these three regulated benefits, the GDR benefits from the overall structure of the trade. During its 1982–1983 cash flow crisis, East Germany was able to buy West German goods, including iron and steel products, for VE and then reexport these goods to the West for hard currency.[28] Furthermore, the strong business relationship between the two Germanys provides the GDR with the ability to overcome short-term planning gaps. Lastly, rather than being barred through protectionist measures, East German exports of textiles, clothing, chemicals, agricultural goods, and refined petroleum products are able to enter and compete in the West German market. As a result, the GDR can import "hard" goods from the West.

Therefore, East Germany will probably be interested in continuing to take advantage of the economic benefits offered by the inter-German trade system. Moreover, the political stigma connected with inter-German trade will be decreased dramatically if East Germany is recognized. Although East Germany probably will continue to diversify its markets as in the past, the further depoliticalization of the relationship between the two Germanys will encourage East Germany to take fuller advantage of the swing credits and to increase the volume of inter-German trade, two steps it has been hesitant to take in the past.[29] For those in the West German government concerned with at least maintaining and then increasing the level of inter-German trade, recognition offers a possible solution.

Conclusion

As there is no way in the near future to change the European status quo short of a major confrontation, the FRG has attempted to preserve the legal concept of the German Reich while working with the GDR to diminish the human costs of the division and to encourage gradual change. This chapter has argued in favor of an agreement among the various players in which West German formal recognition of the GDR would be exchanged for closer links between West Berlin and the FRG. The complicated West German legal theories that continue to bind the German Reich would thus be exchanged for an improvement in the practical relations between the two states. Although the one-nation theory represented an important symbol immediately after Germany's division, since the signing of the Basic Treaty this symbolism has been increasingly lost on the majority of Germans on both sides of the division. The future of *Deutschlandpolitik* lies in deemphasizing political rhetoric and employing quiet diplomacy to achieve substantive acts that will keep the special nature of the German relationship alive in practice rather than in theory.

Notes

1. Judgment of July 31, 1973, Bundesverfassungsgericht (BVerfG), 36 BVerfG 1. Also see *American Journal of International Law* 70 (1976), p. 147.

2. The *Basic Law* is the term applied to the West German constitution.

3. Wilhelm Geck, "Germany and Contemporary International Law," *Texas International Law Journal* 9 (1974), pp. 263, 275; Ulrich Scheuner, "Die staats-rechtliche Stellung der Bundesrepublik," *Die Öffentliche Verwaltung* 17 (1973), p. 581; Hans Heinrich Mahnke, "Rechtsprobleme des Grundlagenvertrages," *Deutschland Archiv* 7 (1974), pp. 130, 131–139.

4. Geck, ibid., p. 265. The German literature on this subject is unending; a few samples include Wilhelm Kewenig, "Deutschlands Rechtslage heute," *Europa-Archiv* 29 (1974), p. 71; Karl Doehring, Wilhelm Kewenig, and Geog. Ress, *Staats und völkerrechtliche Aspekte der Deutschland und Ostpolitik* (New York: Atheneum, 1971), p. 124.

5. Geck, ibid., p. 267.

6. Manfred Zuleeg, "West Germany's Eastern Policy: Legal Claims and Political Realities," *Georgia Journal of International and Comparative Law* 3 (1973), pp. 124–125. This article provides a complete analysis of the *Dachtheorie*.

7. Ibid., p. 130.

8. Scheuner, "Die staatsrechtliche Stellung," p. 583.

9. Greater Berlin refers to all of metropolitan Berlin encompassing present-day East and West Berlin.

10. See Ernest R. Zivier, *The Legal Status of the Land Berlin: A Survey After the Quadripartite Agreement* (Berlin: Berlin Verlag, 1980) pp. 46–47.

11. Ibid., pp. 54–62.

12. The allies' rights pertain mainly to the preservation of public order and the maintenance of the status and security of Berlin, including its economy, trade, and access routes. In theory, however, the allies could be active outside this framework if they deemed it necessary.

13. *International Legal Materials* 10 (1971), p. 895.

14. Zivier, *The Legal Status*, pp. 182–183.

15. *Reichsgesetzblatt* (RGBI), p. 583; *Bundesgesetzblatt* (BGBI) 3, no. 102-1; and *Verordnung über die deutsche Staatsangehörigheit*, February 5, 1934 (RGBI, 1, p. 659; BGBI 3, no. 102-1-1).

16. Gottfried Zieger, "Staatsangehörigkeit im geteilten Deutschland," *Deutschland Archiv* 249 (1972); Zivier, *The Legal Status*, pp. 132–138.

17. Zivier, ibid., pp. 134–135.

18. Andrew Spindler, *The Politics of International Credit* (Washington, D.C.: Brookings Institution, 1984), p. 7.

19. Garland, "Recent Developments in Inter-German Trade and Economic Relations" (Paper presented at the Third World Congress for Soviet and East European Studies, Washington, D.C., October 30–November 4, 1985), p. 23; also see Armin Volze, "Zu den Besonderheiten der innerdeutschen Wirtschaftsbeziehungen im Ost-West-Verhältnis," *Deutsche Studien Sonderdruck* 83.

20. *Die Welt*, December 22, 1982; also see Leslie Colitt, "Bonn's Raw Materials Buy Freedom for East Germans," *Financial Times*, May 23, 1985, p. 2.

21. *Deutschlandpolitik* is the term used by the Federal Republic of Germany to describe its relations with the German Democratic Republic.

22. See Franz Rosch and Fritz Homann, "Thirty Years of the Berlin Agreement— Thirty Years of Inner-German Trade: Economic and Political Dimensions," *Zeitschrift für die gesamte Staatswissenschaft* 137 (1981), pp. 525, 526.

23. EEC Treaty, March 25, 1957, p. 298, United Nations Treaty Series 11 (effective January 1, 1958).

24. Protocol Relating to German Internal Trade and Connected Problems, March 25, 1957, *Bundesgesetzblatt* 2, 984, 298, United Nations Treaty Series 131 [hereinafter referred to as Protocol].

25. *International Legal Materials* 12 (1973), pp. 16, 18.

26. K. Alexander Hobson, "The European Community and East-West German Relations," *Virginia Journal of International Law* 19 (1978), pp. 45, 53.

27. Ehlermann, "Die Entwicklung des innerdeutschen Handels aus der Sicht der europäschen Gemeinschaften," *Deutschland Archiv* 6, Sonderheft 89 (1973), p. 93.

28. See Maria Haendcke-Hoppe, "Konsolidierung in der DDR-Aussenwirtschaft," *Deutschland Archiv* 17 (1984), pp. 1060–1068.

29. In 1957, inter-German trade reached its peak when 11.3 percent of GDR exports went to the FRG. Today, the GDR's exports to West Germany represent approximately 10 percent of its total exports. See Hans J. Jacobson, "The Politics of East-West Trade—the West German Perspective" (Paper presented at the Third World Congress for Soviet and East European Studies, Washington, D.C., October 30–November 4, 1985).

3

A Break with the Past?
The Changing Nature of
East German Foreign Policy

Karin L. Johnston

During the height of the heated debate on the stationing of Pershing and cruise missiles in Europe, a German newspaper quoted its country's leader as admitting that the "unavoidable" decision to deploy more missiles—a necessary act to maintain the global military-strategic balance—"did not evoke jubilation in our country."[1] The comment was not as surprising as the German political leader who made it. Erich Honecker, not Helmut Kohl, made the statement in late November 1983, shortly before the North Atlantic Treaty Organization (NATO) INF deployment took effect. The missile deployment to which Honecker referred was not NATO's, but the upcoming deployment of Soviet missiles in the German Democratic Republic (GDR) and Czechoslovakia. General Secretary Yuri Andropov had just announced the Soviet Union's decision to accelerate the timetable for deployment.

This bold statement in the face of what was then an unalterable Soviet policy decision reflected recent changes in foreign policy activities and style of the GDR. These changes, detectable since the conclusion of West Germany's treaties with the Eastern bloc and the inter-German treaty in the early 1970s, have been most evident in the 1980s. Through these treaties, the international isolation of the GDR has been gradually replaced by growing recognition and internationalization. The Berlin Wall, erected in 1961, has been another factor in the GDR's consolidation. Moreover, mounting economic problems in the early 1980s prompted the GDR increasingly to articulate its own economic and political interests. This process has brought a new self-confidence to the East German leadership and a willingness to express its own national interests in relations with other countries.

This was not always so. Because the majority of the postwar Communist leaderships in Eastern Europe were placed in power by the Soviets, they did not—and to varying extents still do not—possess a strong domestic consensus. Thus, they were dependent on the Soviet Union to maintain the status quo. Soviet-defined bloc policies were seldom questioned. This close relationship was especially important for the East German leadership because of the presence of another German state, the Federal Republic of Germany (FRG), with which it shared deep historical, cultural, and emotional ties. The history of the GDR is punctuated by continual efforts to create its own identity, to establish a separateness from its West German counterpart. East Germans, however, continued to see themselves as "Germans" rather than as "socialists". Consequently, the past few years have witnessed a "resocialization", as it were, of previously unacceptable German historical figures, such as Martin Luther, Frederick the Great, even Otto von Bismarck, to make the interpretation of German history more palatable to a populace that still clings to its German traditions.[2]

Always in the foreground, however, has been—and still remains— one overriding state interest, the stabilization of the political system. Because of the problem of national identity, the GDR leadership is much more reliant on the Soviet Union than are other East European regimes, and thus the relationship with the Soviets remains for the GDR the absolute priority. The GDR has remained fairly stable in the face of recent difficulties in Eastern Europe. The leadership of the Socialist Unity Party (SED) did not encounter the political problems their Soviet counterparts did in the years between Leonid Brezhnev and Mikhail Gorbachev. Nor was the GDR as affected by the general economic downturn in the early 1980s because of its special trade status with the FRG, which provided valuable financial assistance in the form of loans. In addition, its western counterpart also provides a convenient safety valve through which the East German government can rid itself of dissidents and other "undesirables." All these elements have contributed to a relatively stable and increasingly confident regime, and this growing self-confidence has shaped recent events in East German politics.

This chapter looks at the perceptible growth in the GDR's self-confidence and stature as it strives to overcome the vestiges of its past isolation so as to define its national interests in relations with other states. This is discernible not only in the GDR's cultivation of closer ties with nonbloc countries (the United States is used here as an example), but also in the increasing importance of the GDR within the Warsaw Pact and in its relations with its closest and most important ally, the Soviet Union.

But this policy orientation is not without certain risks. The Soviet leadership's decision to punish the West by initiating a freeze in East-West relations after the NATO missile deployment, and its expectation of bloc support for this decision, posed a serious dilemma for the East German government. Reluctant to give up the fruits of détente, particularly with the FRG, Honecker resisted the pressure to follow Moscow's example.

The dispute between East Berlin and Moscow in 1984, in the wake of the NATO missile deployment, reflected the readiness of the SED leadership to stand up to a Soviet policy decision they judged detrimental to the GDR's national interests.[3] Although Honecker was forced by Soviet pressure to cancel his September 1984 visit to the FRG, he did manage to salvage the room for maneuver, or *Handlungsspielraum,* that had been so painstakingly built up during several years. The GDR's limitations, however, were further illustrated by a number of unsuccessful attempts to broaden its policy position, as we shall explore. The SED leadership will continue to test the limits of the GDR's scope for independent initiatives. The question is where the boundaries lie and how the regime can best utilize the *Handlungsspielraum* it gains.

Relations Outside the Bloc

The past few years have witnessed the growing international stature of the GDR. East Berlin has made efforts to cultivate more extensive foreign relations. For example, Honecker has undertaken more official visits to countries outside of the Eastern bloc and encouraged and welcomed visits from a growing number of highly ranked foreign delegations to East Berlin.

Perusal of diplomatic activities in the past few years reflects these trends. In 1983, probably the most important foreign visitor was the U.N. secretary general, Javier Perez de Cuellar. The year 1984 brought more official visits by high-ranking Western officials, including Canada's prime minister, Pierre Trudeau; Italy's prime minister, Bettino Craxi; and Greece's president, Andreas Papandreou. In that same year, Honecker made official visits to Ethiopia, Finland, and Algeria, and Foreign Minister Oskar Fischer was received in Spain, Austria, and Mexico.[4] The pace continued in 1985, with Honecker visiting Italy and hosting Britain's foreign minister, Sir Geoffrey Howe; France's prime minister, Laurent Fabius; Japan's foreign minister, Shiutaro Abe; and Finland's president, Kalevi Sorsa. More state occasions followed in 1986, including a much-publicized visit by Honecker to Sweden.

Clearly the most crucial visit for the SED leadership, however, was Honecker's historic visit to the Federal Republic of Germany in September 1987. The visit had been postponed three times. But a favorable atmosphere between the superpowers made this planned visit less contingent on the exigencies of East-West relations as had been the case previously.

Protocol was an especially sensitive matter for Bonn.[5] The question of how to receive the East German leader without giving credence to the SED's long-sought policy objective of establishing GDR sovereignty in the eyes of the world was critical to the debate in the FRG. In the end, a concession to pomp and circumstance—complete with flags and national hymns—was the price Bonn paid in exchange for GDR cooperation on other issues, including the easing of travel restrictions for East Germans under sixty-five years of age.

The Federal Chancellory, as well as many conservative officials and observers, went to great lengths to assert that it was not a state visit but a "normal working visit," the difference being that the federal president had not extended the invitation.[6] Few were convinced. Most felt the visit was a *de facto* recognition of East-West German realities— "an end to all illusions of reunification"[7] and a confirmation of the existence of two sovereign German states. The visit heralded no great changes in inner-German relations, but it did bring the GDR one step closer to its goal of building its own separate identity. More importantly for the SED leadership, the way was now open for diplomatic initiatives in London, Paris, and Washington, the important missing links in its efforts to expand relations outside of the Eastern bloc.

The GDR's new efforts to build bilateral ties with nonbloc countries can be seen in the upsurge of U.S.–East German relations since the early 1980s.[8] The GDR was never perceived as an independent political actor by U.S. policymakers; rather, it was always viewed through the prism of U.S.–West German or Soviet-U.S. relations. In this sense, the GDR was the square peg that did not fit in the more rounded political configurations of the West European or East European geopolitical arenas.

Official U.S. recognition of the GDR came only in 1974, and relations between the two states did not move perceptibly during the next decade. Before then, Western analysts tended to view the GDR as part of the East European "monolith"—orthodox and dogmatic, bound inextricably to the Soviet Union. The GDR did little to dispel this view. The events surrounding the 1983 missile deployment in Western Europe, in which the position of the East German leadership was anything but an automatic acceptance and implementation of Moscow's policies, reflected the GDR's altered status.

Recent changes in East German foreign policy have encouraged contacts between the GDR and the United States. Such changes appear to fit well into the broader framework of U.S. interests, and, as Anita Mallinckrodt pointed out,[9] they accord with the increased U.S. interest in developing its bilateral relations with the states of Eastern Europe.

Current U.S. interest in the GDR is reflected in Washington's East European policy of differentiation—that is, supporting individual states in their attempts to gain a measure of independence from the Soviet Union.[10] Although differentiation has been an element of U.S. foreign policy since the 1960s, it commanded more attention during the Reagan administration. Broadly speaking, the policy is aimed at limiting Soviet influence in Eastern Europe by promoting human rights, encouraging trade and financial arrangements with Western countries, and supporting reform and decentralization initiatives. The long-term goal of the policy is to maintain U.S. interests in Europe while attempting to curtail Soviet activities there as well.

The U.S. position vis-à-vis the GDR can be viewed as a two-pronged approach. Officially, Washington has always encouraged good relations between the two German states. Successive U.S. administrations have recognized that every West German government, regardless of political color, has a continuing, and legal, commitment to protect and improve relations with East Germany. It must be added, however, that Washington's support of inner-German relations will continue only so long as such relations are not perceived as endangering West Germany's NATO membership.

Paralleling its support of inner-German relations is Washington's effort to improve bilateral relations with the GDR. In January 1984, an advance team was sent to East Berlin to prepare for the February visit of Richard Burt, then assistant secretary of state for European and Canadian affairs in the State Department and the highest ranking U.S. official to visit the GDR up to that time.[11] Other visits from State Department officials and congresspersons followed, culminating in the October 4, 1984, meeting between Secretary of State George Shultz and GDR Foreign Minister Oskar Fischer in New York. There is some support in the United States for expanding relations with the GDR through better trade relations. There are also potential obstacles, such as the GDR's pursuit of most-favored-nation status, given the reluctance of the United States to extend government-subsidized loans to countries with such questionable discriminatory practices as denying citizens the right to emigrate.

Material claims negotiations are another aspect of the GDR's drive to expand its relations with the United States. Negotiations between the GDR and the Conference on Jewish Material Claims on the issue of compensation for Jewish property expropriated during the Nazi era have recently been renewed and are showing positive movement. The United States and the GDR have also conducted negotiations on a monetary payment for U.S. government property and the property of

U.S. citizens expropriated by the East Germans after 1945.[12] No agreements have yet been reached on these matters, but the existence of such negotiations reflects an improvement, as least for the time being, in East German–U.S. relations.

There are obvious advantages for the GDR in building relations with the United States. Politically, the East German leadership would thereby continue the process of internationalization that began with West Germany's *Ostpolitik* and the concomitant abandonment of the Hallstein Doctrine (Bonn's declared policy from 1955 to 1968 to sever diplomatic relations with states that recognized the GDR). Economic relations with the West will continue to be cultivated to the benefit not only of the East Germans but of the Soviets as well. The Soviet Union is hardly opposed to such contacts because of its need for the more technologically sophisticated industrial goods furnished by the GDR, its most important trade partner. But in order to improve its level of technological sophistication, the GDR is reliant on the West to provide the needed technology. Thus, cultivating good political and economic relations with the FRG and the West is essential to the SED leadership.

Despite the hard rhetoric aimed at the United States in the past, the GDR is presently giving different signals on the diplomatic level. The interest of the U.S. government, seen recently in the cautious and limited overtures to East Berlin, will certainly not diminish in the immediate future, given the increasing political and economic weight of the GDR in the Warsaw Pact and with other countries outside the Eastern bloc. As its importance vis-à-vis its Warsaw Pact partners increases, the GDR is in a better position to articulate and defend its own interests within that forum. The GDR is, in short, pursuing a more expanded foreign policy—an "expanded realism of foreign policy activity," as Hanns-Dieter Jacobsen has observed.[13] The relative improvement of relations between the United States and the GDR is precisely that—there has been a relative improvement in the political climate but no rapprochement. Sensitive items on the U.S.–East German agenda, such as the claims negotiations and the continuing U.S. defense of the four-power status of the entire city of Berlin, do not promise any rapid or significant advancements in bilateral relations.

Bloc Relations

Relations between the Soviet Union and East Germany are still influenced by the legacy of World War II and the years of military occupation that followed. The GDR is strategically and militarily vital to the Soviet Union, and although there are constant reminders of the "eternal friendship" between the two states,[14] elements of Soviet distrust still exist. An interesting example of this distrust is the GDR's military position within the Warsaw Pact. The German text of the Warsaw Treaty implies that the extent and direction of East Germany's military assistance are determined by the other member states. Furthermore, the inclusion of the entire Nationale Volksarmee (NVA) in the Warsaw Pact's joint force effectively places the East German troops at the full disposal of the Soviet-controlled Supreme Command.

Another example is the 1957 Soviet–East German Treaty on the Stationing of Soviet Troops in the GDR, which regulates the presence of the former Soviet occupation troops stationed on East German soil. The treaty does not allow the East Germans a voice in determining troop strength, deployment, or movement—they may only "advise." The Soviet supreme commander may adopt any measure deemed necessary should the Warsaw Pact troops be "at risk" (the general clause reads "in the event of a threat to security").[15] The Soviet Union, in effect, exercises significant influence on East Germany's security affairs, which amounts to a substantial restriction of GDR sovereignty.

The Soviet Union also perpetuates its influence in the GDR through its ongoing status as a victorious ally in the anti-Hitler coalition. The Soviet presence in the GDR is based on the rights and privileges of a victor power (*Siegerrecht*), not on any agreement between the two states. Moscow would veto any moves affecting this status. Moreover, the GDR's vital geostrategic location (to which twenty Soviet divisions attest) will continue to afford it a special place in Soviet political calculations.

Perhaps even more importantly, the GDR's political and economic stability has made it the Soviet Union's most important bloc partner—in contrast to Poland, which, because of the Solidarity movement and the country's cyclical political and economic crises, has become a less reliable ally for Moscow.[16] East Berlin has also proven to be an effective tool for reminding other East European governments of the necessity for bloc discipline. Through its strong support not only of the Kremlin's foreign policies but of bloc policies as well, the GDR has established itself as a loyal and dependable ally. Thus, the reliability of the GDR, manifested in its political stability and economic strength, has served to raise its stature within Eastern Europe. Whether or not this process will continue, however, and what degree of influence East Berlin will exercise in the future are open to speculation.

In recent years, the contours of a new policy development and coordination in which the GDR has pursued its own national interests on a number of fronts have been perceptible. The growing self-confidence of a leadership no longer willing to completely subordinate its interests was illustrated in spring and summer 1984, in the wake of the Euromissile debate and the deployment of Pershing II and ground-launched cruise

missiles in Western Europe. The Soviet Union adopted a hard line with
the West after an intensive propaganda campaign aimed at dividing the
NATO alliance failed to dissuade the West Europeans from accepting
deployment of U.S. missiles on their soil.

The GDR, however, was well aware that it, more than any other
Warsaw Pact country, would have to shoulder the weight of a freeze in
relations with the West, given its close economic and financial ties with
the FRG and its dependence on continued economic success for the
regime's stability. The necessity of dialogue rather than confrontation
was clearly perceived by the SED leadership. Accordingly, Honecker
developed a policy of *Schadensbegrenzung* (damage limitation) and called
for a return to détente. These initiatives brought the GDR into a position
diametrically opposed to Moscow.[17] Although the process of policy
decisionmaking in Eastern bloc states is not known to Western observers,
there can be no doubt that differences among the party elite do arise
and as such are dealt with behind closed doors. What was unusual in
this case was that the dispute between the Soviet Union and the GDR
simmered until it broke the surface and continued to be openly played
out.

The concept of *Handlungsspielraum* was much discussed in relation
to the East German initiatives during the dispute.[18] Perhaps the essence
of the controversy can best be summed up in the following question:
Can smaller Eastern bloc states, playing an intermediary role, positively
impact on the international climate during times of tension between the
superpowers? A negative response would rule out all possibilities of
exerting any degree of influence during periods of superpower tension.
As a consequence, the smaller states would be compelled to fully support
the Soviet Union's position in the formulation of their own foreign policy,
thus limiting their sphere of action. An affirmative response would imply
that because the Soviet Union is so focused on the conflict with its
superpower opponent, its allies would have greater opportunity to seek
and attain more flexibility in their external relations.

The answer, as so often is the case, lies somewhere in the middle.[19]
It is not a question of whether the smaller bloc states do or do not
possess any room for maneuver because, fundamentally, each East
European leadership has a spectrum of policy responses. But the breadth
of their *Handlungsspielraum* is dependent on the ebbs and flows of East-
West relations. This dynamic has at times proven resilient enough for
the smaller East European states to formulate their individual policy
goals and incorporate them into the decisionmaking process of the
alliance system.

There are, however, clear limits to the policy of *Handlungsspielraum*.
On some issues, such as the dominant status of the Soviet Union within

the Eastern bloc, virtually no flexibility exists. Thus, as the GDR attempts to expand the boundaries of its policy initiatives at various levels of interaction—within the bloc, with nonbloc countries, and with Bonn—the SED leadership is well aware that extensive autonomy from the Soviet Union is not feasible.

Testing the Scope of Policy Initiatives

The development of the GDR from a passive to a more active and self-confident political actor was discernible in the 1984 controversy between Moscow and East Berlin.[20] The conflict manifested itself in the relations between East and West Germany and eventually focused on Erich Honecker's planned visit to West Germany in September 1984. The real point of discord, however, lay not in the *Deutschlandpolitik*. Rather, it was in the diverging perceptions of the Soviet Union and its major bloc allies concerning the appropriate response of the Warsaw Pact to NATO's decision to deploy Pershing II and cruise missiles in Europe (the dual-track decision). The issue was whether they should pursue a policy of détente or adopt a more uncompromising political line.

Above all, the dispute touched on one of Moscow's dominant political-strategic priorities—maintaining bloc cohesion. What Moscow demanded from its allies was complete fealty toward a strategy designed to punish the West by freezing relations;[21] but several Warsaw Pact states—notably the GDR—balked at such a decision. For the SED, too much was at stake if it severed political and economic relations with the West. The dispute reflected not so much a fracture in the foundation of the bloc system as a disagreement on the tactics of a particular policy. For neither the existence of the Warsaw Pact nor the dominance of the Soviet Union in Eastern Europe had been called into question.

The Background of the Dispute

The issues at the core of the dispute had their genesis during Yuri Andropov's short term in office as general secretary of the Communist Party of the Soviet Union (CPSU). Recognizing the failure of the Soviet model as an effective catalyst for economic growth and efficiency, Andropov sought to alleviate the pressure on the Soviet economy by handing more responsibility for economic decisions over to its Warsaw Pact partners, a kind of "national" search for the solutions to Eastern Europe's economic woes. In an April 1982 speech, Andropov stated that the best model for each state to follow was one not only publicly acceptable but also consistent with its own traditions and interests.[22]

The effect of that pronouncement was a broadening of the *Handlungs-spielraum* for each regime in the bloc. Soviet acquiescence in Honecker's exercise of greater flexibility in policy formation reflected Andropov's calculation that given its extremely close relationship with the Soviet Union, a more confident and autonomous GDR posed no risk. The protracted succession crises, which weakened Soviet leadership, also contributed to this window of opportunity for the SED. Indeed, the lack of consensus in the Kremlin opened up possibilities for all of its East European allies to articulate and pursue policies more in their national interests.

But the unsettled leadership crisis also served to strengthen the hard-liners in the CPSU, who demanded a confrontational approach to the West. Their strength was revealed in the Politburo's decision to break off the intermediate-range nuclear forces (INF) negotiations in Geneva and initiate a "revanchist" campaign aimed primarily at the FRG.[23] For the Soviets, the charge of revanchism generally serves two purposes. First, it is, as Ronald Asmus described, a "time-honored weapon in Moscow's arsenal of political psychological warfare,"[24] usually directed at the West Germans in an attempt to influence policy decisions in Bonn. In 1984, revanchist charges were amplified in order to curtail what Moscow perceived to be overly friendly ties between the German states and to "punish" the FRG for accepting NATO missiles. Second, such charges serve to enforce bloc discipline and strengthen bloc cohesion. In 1984, the Soviet Union issued a series of warnings to East Berlin and its other allies not to stray from the defined Soviet policy line. The key for the Soviets at the time appeared to be Bonn, for if Bonn could be persuaded to dismantle the missiles, it would constitute a defeat for NATO and U.S. policy in Europe—hence, Moscow's political and pro-pagandistic pressure on the FRG and the call for a united front in the Soviet policy of confrontation.

Foreign Minister Andrei Gromyko had made clear in October 1983 that the Soviets were preparing to take "countermeasures" against the NATO INF deployment.[25] Yet, in November, *Neues Deutschland* printed a speech given by Honecker at the SED's Seventh Central Committee Plenum in which, in a surprisingly open manner, he admitted that the Soviet countermeasures—the deployment of operational-tactical missiles in the GDR and Czechoslovakia—were not popular in the GDR. He also stated that the GDR favored "limiting the damage as much as possible."[26] This policy of *Schadensbegrenzung* explicitly supported the road of détente and was clearly at odds with the Soviet hard-line position.

These differences increasingly manifested themselves in the press. In a January 1984 interview for the French weekly *Revolution*, Honecker supported the position that relations between the two Germanys should continue to develop within a European framework of treaties.[27] Past treaties, therefore, were to remain the basis for future GDR ties. At the same time, Radio Moscow was proclaiming that the decision to station the Euromissiles in the FRG had shown that country's politics to be incalculable and its declaration of peace to be "unbelievable."[28] To Moscow, any expressed Western interest in dialogue was mere deception.

The SED leadership indirectly defended its position by printing two articles in *Neues Deutschland* by the Hungarian Communist party secretary responsible for foreign affairs, Mátyás Szűrös.[29] In those articles, Szűros emphasized the importance of the "national" over the "international" interests of a country, envisioning a definite role in world affairs for small countries in the form of bringing differences of views together and developing "rational and mutually acceptable compromises."[30] Small and medium-sized states could, in a supportive role, assist in defusing international tensions and furthering the cause of détente.[31] The Szűros articles did not so much posit a new "theory" on the role of small states in the Eastern bloc as reflect the weakness of Soviet leadership and the growing self-awareness of its bloc allies at that time. Thus, because there were no clear directives from Moscow, a situation developed in which the smaller bloc countries attempted to assert themselves more forcefully in their policy orientations.

The spring of 1984 brought progressively critical commentaries from the Soviet media on what were termed the revanchist policies of the FRG.[32] The reaction of the SED, however, was reserved. It did not immediately join in or endorse the polemics. When it did, the response was publication of a shortened, edited excerpt of the Soviet text together with a comparatively mild comment. The unmistakable message was that East Berlin was not going to sacrifice the economic and financial advantages of inner-German relations to accommodate Soviet anxieties. While allegations of revanchist and militarist tendencies in the Federal Republic rebounded in Soviet newspapers, the East German press printed speeches by Honecker reaffirming his policy of damage limitation and calling for the two German states to form a "community of responsibility" to address the problems of world peace and European security.[33]

Since coming to power, the Kohl government had attempted to counteract Soviet charges of revanchism by making clear to East Berlin that it would be "business as usual" in the inner-German discussion; no major changes in *Deutschlandpolitik* were to be undertaken.[34] To underscore this position, Bonn agreed in July of 1984 to guarantee a second major loan to the GDR. In return, the GDR would alleviate a number of travel restrictions, effective August 1, 1984.[35] Thus, both German states signaled their intent to maintain, and even expand, the inner-German dialogue despite Moscow's uneasiness.

The Soviets, in fact, were not pleased by the negotiations that continued on such issues as cultural exchanges, environmental issues, and East German emigration, nor were they comfortable with the plethora of meetings between East and West German officials concerning the up-coming Honecker visit. For Moscow, the German-German détente was proceeding at too alarming a rate. A series of articles in *Pravda* warned the GDR against expanding relations with West Germany, noting that relations "between the two German states cannot be viewed in isolation from the entire international situation."[36] The postponement of Honecker's visit eventually proved unavoidable. As Moscow continued with its drumbeat denunciations of West Germany and bald warning as to its "veto" position regarding continuation of the East-West German dialogue, cancellation of the visit became only a question of time and circumstance.

The pretext was provided when Alfred Dregger, the Christian Democratic Union parliamentary floor leader, announced in an August 23 interview in *Die Welt* that "the future of the Federal Republic does not depend upon whether Mr. Honecker pays us the honor of his visit."[37] *Neues Deutschland* charged that these remarks were a conscious attempt to sabotage East-West relations,[38] and further editorials pointed to a hardening of East Berlin's official line. On September 4, Ewald Moldt, the GDR diplomatic envoy in Bonn, informed the Kohl government that Honecker's visit to the FRG would no longer take place as arranged, due ostensibly to Dregger's untimely remark. Although the immediate controversy between Moscow and East Berlin had in effect been settled, the broader question of the role of the Soviet Union's allies within the bloc and in relations outside of the Warsaw Pact was left unanswered.

Other Independent Initiatives

Although the GDR leadership realizes that the opportunity for independent policy initiatives in fundamental issues is limited, it has nevertheless "tested" its scope of maneuverability in other ways as well. One such instance involved the official designation of Soviet troops in East Germany, known as the Group of Soviet Forces in Germany, or GSFG.[39] In May 1985, *Neues Deutschland* unexpectedly began to refer to the Soviet troops as the Group of Soviet Forces in the GDR, a serious move because the semantic change implied that the Soviet presence and influence no longer applied to all of Germany but only to that part designated as the GDR. The commander in chief of the Soviet armed forces demanded and received an immediate retraction from *Neues Deutschland* of its choice of words and a reaffirmation of the original designation.

Another clash took place on a wintry night in November 1984. At midnight on November 15, the Glienicke bridge between West Berlin and Potsdam, used only by members of the Western allies' military missions in Potsdam and, due to their status, normally subject only to Soviet controls, was closed by East German border guards.[40] The catalyst for this action was a stalemated negotiation concerning the financing of bridge repairs in which East German officials demanded that the city of West Berlin also assume repair costs to that part of the bridge in the GDR. When the East Germans announced their intention to close the bridge, the Western allies pressured the Soviet Union (which maintains its own military missions in the three western zones of Germany under a four-power agreement going back to 1947) to assist in the resolution of the conflict. But the GDR remained firm in its decision and blocked the bridge at midnight on November 15. By 9:00 A.M. on November 16, however, the Western allies were informed by the Soviet ambassador in East Berlin that the bridge would reopen at noon. Again, the Soviet Union lost no time in quashing action impacting on its political-military status in the GDR and in Germany as a whole.

The third event concerned the GDR's decision in May 1986 to initiate new pass requirements for diplomats traveling between the eastern and western sectors of Berlin. On Thursday, May 22, the East German government announced that beginning Monday, May 26, diplomats traveling from East Berlin to West Berlin would be required to show passports in addition to the diplomatic identification passes issued by the East German Foreign Ministry.[41] Ostensibly, such steps were being taken in response to Western pleas for the implementation of measures to fight the spread of terrorism in the wake of the April 1986 bombing of the La Belle disco in West Berlin. Two people were killed, one of them a U.S. soldier. The assumption in the West was that the terrorists, with the support of the GDR government, had first taken cover in East Berlin and from there had crossed over to the western sector of the city.

A showing of passports would be, in effect, an acknowledgement not of a demarcation line between different sectors of the city, but of a border between two separate states. Under the 1971 Four-Power Agreement on the status of Berlin, sector boundaries are defined as demarcation lines within the city, whereas the East German legal interpretation is that the boundary between the three western sectors and the eastern sector constitutes a state border between the GDR and West Berlin. To defeat the GDR's purpose, Western diplomats made large detours from East Berlin and entered West Berlin through GDR border crossings, where passports had always been required.

The matter was, from the beginning, a four-power dispute because of its severe implications for the status of Berlin.[42] The Soviet Union, however, remained surprisingly subdued during the course of the dispute, never publicly defending the position of its bloc partner. As the Western allies showed their resolve to oppose the new regulations, it became clear that the Soviet Union was unwilling to support the East German case. The deadlock ended with the East German government announcing the introduction of a new diplomatic identification pass and quietly dropping all mention of the passport requirement.[43] The whole episode ended not with a bang, but a whimper, and not without a loss of face for East Berlin.

The dispute had its share of odd turns and contradictions. The disco bombing and the U.S. call for security measures to prevent future terrorist activities were cited by East Berlin as justification for the new passport regulations. The East German government must have observed with satisfaction as the West Berlin police, at the urging of the Western allies, initiated a passport control in the wake of the La Belle bombing on all West Berlin public transportation lines that ran through East Berlin and back into the western sector of the city. This initiative implicitly acknowledged an inner-city border and could be cited by the East Germans as a precedent to establish their own "border controls." Yet during the entire diplomatic passport conflict, the East German guards had been instructed not to demand passports from the U.S., British, and French diplomats.[44] By exempting the three Western powers from the passport requirement the GDR had, on its side, indirectly recognized and underscored the four-power status of Berlin as a whole and acknowledged the existence of allied rights in all four sectors of the city.[45]

The motives of the East German action remain unclear, for any change of policy affecting the status of Berlin also impinges not only on the rights of the three Western powers but on the Soviet Union's rights as an occupation power as well. Some observers claim East Berlin acted on directives from Moscow; others argue the initial plan originated in East Berlin, albeit with Moscow's approval.[46] But the questions remain: Did the GDR receive promises of support, only to find that support withdrawn in the last minute? Was the Soviet Union not entirely averse to seeing that the GDR's nose got a little bloodied, if only to bring Honecker back into line—or at least to point out to the East Germans that they were still dependent on Moscow to avoid such future debacles? Or, ultimately, was the degree of Western solidarity simply underestimated? These questions are, of course, a matter of speculation. It does not seem likely, however, that East Berlin acted without the prior knowledge of Soviet leaders, given the "status" implications of its action.

Whatever the case, it is puzzling that in the move to ensure more flexibility and maneuverability in policy responses—and, importantly, in the effort to gain more popular acceptance by underscoring the GDR's separate identity—the SED leadership would choose a line of action that was more risk laden and prone to failure than other subjects or targets. Perhaps the nascent self-confidence prompted attempts to eliminate the more manifest obstacles to its international sovereignty, even if there was little confidence for success.

Conclusion

Efforts to gain more *Handlungsspielraum* reflect the constant balancing act the SED leadership must perform. On the one hand, it is dependent on the support of the Soviet Union without whose political benevolence and military presence it could not survive. On the other hand, it requires a modicum of popular support that can only be attained by distancing the GDR, at least to an extent, from the Soviet Union. Some may argue the GDR regime requires no popular consent, that it could rely on established institutional watchdogs to assure compliance. But in the political game of choice between the carrot and the stick, it is always more advantageous for a government to rule with the tacit acquiescence, if not active support, of its populace.

Honecker's comments on the lack of "jubilation" at the Soviet Union's announcement of a new missile deployment in the GDR reflected popular dissatisfaction with the decision and the popularity and widespread support of Honecker's policy of *Schadensbegrenzung* among East Germans. The GDR's attempt to limit the negative fallout from the Soviets' hardline policy and preserve hard-earned maneuvering room in the diplomatic field reflects the SED's new approach to domestic and foreign policy initiatives. The failure of some of these initiatives points to ongoing limitations on the GDR's *Handlungsspielraum* within the Soviet bloc. The overall thrust of East German diplomacy, however, indicates that the GDR will continue to test these limitations and push for the expansion of its *Handlungsspielraum* in an effort to increase its stature in the international arena.

Notes

1. *Neues Deutschland*, November 26–27, 1983, p. 3.

2. Walter Leisler Kiep, "The New Deutschlandpolitik," *Foreign Affairs* (Winter 1984-1985), p. 312. More specifically, see Ronald Asmus, "The GDR and Martin Luther," *Survey* 28, no. 3 (Autumn 1984), pp. 124–156.

3. For a general discussion see Ronald Asmus, *East Berlin and Moscow: The Documentation of a Dispute* (Munich: Radio Free Europe, 1985).

4. Ronald Asmus, "The Dialectics of Detente and Discord: The Moscow–East Berlin–Bonn Triangle," *Orbis* (Winter 1985), p. 751.

5. See such articles as *Süddeutsche Zeitung*, July 15, 1987, p. 1; *Der Spiegel* 36 (1987), p. 20; and Peter Jochen Winters, "Erich Honecker in der Bundesrepublik," *Deutschland Archiv* (October 1987), pp. 1009–1010.

6. *Süddeutsche Zeitung,* July 17, 1987, p. 1.

7. *Der Spiegel* 36 (1987), p. 22.

8. Ronald Asmus, "Bonn und Ost-Berlin aus Washingtoner Sicht," *Deutschland Archiv* (March 1985), p. 256.

9. Anita Mallinckrodt, "Bonn und Ost-Berlin: andere Sichten aus Washington," *Deutschland Archiv* (April ;1985), p. 389.

10. Hanns-Dieter Jacobsen, "Rapprochement Between the United States and the German Democratic Republic?" *German Studies Newsletter,* no. 5 (June 1985), p. 19. A more recent discussion of differentiation in the East European context is F. Stephen Larrabee, "Eastern Europe: A Generational Change," *Foreign Policy,* no. 70 (Spring 1988), pp. 42–64.

11. Asmus, "Bonn und Ost-Berlin," p. 261.

12. Jacobsen, "Rapprochement," p. 18.

13. Ibid., p. 20.

14. This is underscored in the 1974 Constitution of the GDR, Article 6 paragraph (2), which reads: "The German Democratic Republic is forever and irrevocably allied with the Union of Soviet Socialist Republics" (translation by author).

15. Melvin Croan, "Development of the GDR Political Relations with the USSR," in E. Schultz et al., *GDR Foreign Policy* (Armonk, N.Y.: M. E. Sharpe, 1982), pp. 221–222.

16. Interview with Stefan Goebel, Director of the Office of GDR Foreign Policy Research in the FRG Permanent Mission in East Berlin on January 22, 1986. Also see ibid., p. 186.

17. *Neues Deutschland,* November 26–27, 1983, p. 3.

18. See such articles as Arnulf Baring, "Wieviel Spielraum hat die DDR?" *Frankfurter Allgemeine Zeitung,* October 3, 1985, p. 1; Fred Oldenburg, "Werden Moskaus Schatten länger?" *Deutschland Archiv* (August 1984), pp. 834–843; and Fred Oldenburg, "Geht die SED eigene Wege im Sowjetimperium?" *Deutschland Archiv* (May 1984), pp. 491–496.

19. Peter Danylow, "Der aussenpolitische Spielraum der DDR," *Europa Archiv,* no. 14 (1985), p. 440.

20. See Asmus, *East Berlin and Moscow;* and Johannes Kuppe's report in *Der Konflikt zwischen DDR und UdSSR über die Deutschlandpolitik im Jahre 1984,* Analysen und Berichte no. 12 (Bonn: Gesamtdeutsches Institut, Bundesanstalt für gesamtdeutsche Aufgaben, 1985), pp. 1–20.

21. Kuppe, ibid., p. 15.

22. Lothar Jung, "Zum Konflikt DDR-UdSSR," *Deutschland Archiv* (April 1985), p. 393.

23. Ibid., p. 394.

24. Asmus, *East Berlin and Moscow,* p. 11.

25. *Neues Deutschland,* October 18, 1983, p. 3.

26. *Neues Deutschland,* November 26–27, 1983, p. 3.

27. *Neues Deutschland,* January 6, 1984, p. 3.

28. Radio Moscow, January 9, 1984, as quoted in Kuppe, *Der Konflikt,* p. 42.

29. *Neues Deutschland,* April 12, 1984, p. 5–6.

30. Ibid., p. 6.

31. Ibid.

32. See the following articles and commentaries reprinted in Asmus, *East Berlin and Moscow*, pp. 46, 53, 74, and 75. See also *Der Konflikt*," pp. 64, 94, and 98.

33. *Neues Deutschland*, August 18–19, 1984, p. 1.

34. Asmus, "The Dialectics," p. 747.

35. Ibid., pp. 750–751, 759.

36. Asmus, *East Berlin and Moscow*, p. 72 (translated by author).

37. *Die Welt*, August 23, 1984, p. 1.

38. *Neues Deutschland*, August 25–26, 1984, p. 1.

39. "Gruppe sowjetischer Streitkräfte in Deutschland," *DDR Handbuch* (Köln: Bundesministerium für innerdeutsche Beziehungen, Verlag Wissenschaft und Politik, 1985), p. 587.

40. *Neue Zuercher Zeitung*, November 16, 1985, p. 3.

41. *Tagesspiegel*, May 25, 1986, p. 2.

42. *Tagesspiegel*, May 28, 1986, p. 1.

43. *Süddeutsche Zeitung*, June 2, 1986, p. 4.

44. *Tagesspiegel*, May 29, 1986, p. 1.

45. *Süddeutsche Zeitung*, June 2, 1986, p. 4.

46. Ibid.

4

Inter-German Relations: Has the Cost Risen for the West?

Sandra E. Peterson

Most of the studies dealing with the inter-German economic relationship assume that the West Germans do not need this "special" relationship as much as the East Germans do.[1] Although it is true that West Germany does not gain significantly from this relationship on economic grounds, the events since 1981 call for a rethinking of this basic assumption. Almost all prior analyses of inter-German relations have emphasized that the West has had the advantage in negotiating with the German Democratic Republic (GDR) and that the West has been quite generous in providing economic assistance.

As the standard argument goes, the Federal Republic of Germany (FRG) provided aid to the East most often on humanitarian grounds to better the conditions of its "brothers" in the East.[2] Furthermore, the West had little stake in this relationship besides securing access and stability for West Berlin. East Germany, on the other hand, gained economically and politically from this relationship.[3] It gained economically through the large infusion of deutsche marks and the interest-free credits provided for trade. Politically, after the signing of the Basic Treaty in 1971, the East Germans gained international recognition from more than one hundred governments, and the increased standard of living made possible through FRG generosity decreased domestic dissatisfaction with the regime. Although this analysis of inter-German relations may be correct for the 1970s, it is no longer an adequate assessment on the dynamics of this relationship in the 1980s.

One of the central reasons given for the East German dependence on the German-German relationship is political-economic. The GDR's political legitimacy is frequently considered a function of its ability to provide its citizens with consumer goods and a higher standard of living than its East European allies. But the basis of GDR legitimacy may also be changing. The country has weathered its exposure to the West (particularly through relative contact and West German television), and it has rediscovered its history.[4] Its position within the Eastern bloc as the most stable and prosperous country also provided its citizens with a sense of pride.[5] Moreover, Erich Honecker's attempts in 1984 to distance the GDR somewhat from the Soviet line has furthered the legitimacy of the GDR government.[6] Most East Germans do not believe that a quick change in their government is possible. They are aware of their government's limits in steering a new course. But there does seem to be a feeling that the government is trying to do what it can with its limited room for maneuver (*Spielraum*), something that probably could not be said ten years ago.

On the other side of the Berlin Wall, we have also seen a change. This has, ironically, become most evident after the *Wende* (turnaround) in Bonn from a Left-Center to a Right-Center government. The present West German government needs a good relationship with East Berlin as much or more than its predecessor did in order to maintain support. Indeed, the Right needs to show more clearly its support for inter-German détente because it is more closely scrutinized by the press and the populace. Good inter-German relations are taken for granted in West Germany now, and politically, the government cannot afford to be responsible for its demise.[7]

How and why has the balance shifted in inter-German relations? What are the underlying political and economic factors behind this shift? First, an examination of the GDR economy reveals that although the East needs West German economic assistance, it is not wholly dependent upon West Germany for its political legitimacy and economic stability. Second, an examination of the four crucial negotiations between Bonn and East Berlin in the 1980s shows that the East German regime has exacted an increasingly higher price for the concessions it has made to Bonn. The most recent negotiations concerning political refugees coming into West Berlin via the GDR is the most interesting and shows most clearly that the East Berliners have gained a lot of leverage in dealing with the government in Bonn. Negative linkage has rarely been an effective tool for Bonn to use in extracting concessions out of East Berlin, but the cost of its positive linkage policy has grown during the years, as its stake in the negotiations has grown. "Whatever their political difference both see the continuation of the *Deutschlandpolitik* as being in Germany's national interest."[8]

The GDR Economy: How Healthy Is It
and How Much Does It Need the FRG?

The GDR economy is the most successful, specialized, and technologically advanced of all of the members of the Council of Mutual Economic Assistance (CMEA). According to the World Bank, the GDR is the twelfth-ranked industrialized country in the world and has the highest per capita income among the socialist countries.[9] It is, however, a country with few natural resources and as a consequence has been historically dependent upon exports, as has the FRG.[10] As a percentage of gross domestic product, East German exports account for more than 25 percent, as is the case in the FRG. But, unlike West Germany after World War II, the East German economy faced far worse conditions because of reparation payments to the USSR and the total dismantling of industries. Despite these disadvantages, the GDR has seen impressive annual growth rates. Indeed, "the FRG and GDR economies grew at roughly the same rate between 1960 and 1973, at a respectable rate of approximately 4.5 percent per annum."[11] However, although the GDR started from a much worse economic base than the FRG, during the past twenty years the East Germans have received huge explicit and implicit subsidies from the Soviet Union—on average double the amount of any other CMEA country.[12] Particularly in the area of energy and other raw materials, these subsidies have alleviated many of the country's economic difficulties.

In addition to economic assistance from the USSR, most analysts attribute the GDR's relative economic health to its close ties to the FRG. It is true that the signing of the Basic Treaty and the "normalization" of inter-German relations greatly benefited the GDR in the 1970s and that a certain level of dependence on this relationship was necessary to maintain growth rates of 4 percent, but the GDR, through a concerted strategy, diminished this dependence in the 1980s. As the East German dependence on the FRG declines so will Bonn's ability to use positive linkage in order to gain political concessions from East Berlin. An overview of inter-German economic relations in the 1970s and 1980s illustrates this point.

The 1970s

In the 1970s, the GDR economy continued to grow at an impressive rate. In the early 1970s, net material product grew by approximately 5 percent and reached more than 6 percent in 1975. In the second half of the 1970s, growth slowed somewhat but still grew on average at about 3.5–4.0 percent per annum.[13] In terms of standard of living,

consumer durable consumption, and social welfare policies, major ex-
pansions in all three areas occurred in the 1970s.[14] Much of the improvement in the economy during this period can be attributed to
economic relations with the West, particularly with West Germany. GDR
trade with the USSR declined during this period. From 1970 to 1974,
the proportion of GDR total trade with the USSR dropped from 39.1
percent to 31.4 percent; at the same time, trade with the West increased
from 24.4 percent to 30.9 percent.[15] Through 1980, GDR trade with the
West fluctuated around 25–26 percent.

During the 1970s, much of the increase in trade with the West and
financial credits came from the FRG. Indeed, the exchange of goods
between the GDR and the FRG exceeded GDR trade with all other
Western industrialized countries combined. The East German economy
benefited enormously from its special relationship with the FRG. "Between
1970 and 1977, the total of swing credits, visa charges, minimum foreign
exchange requirements for visitors, toll roads and other fees amounted
to a cumulative DM 7.5 billion paid by the FRG to the GDR."[16] This
figure does not include direct transfers from relatives in the West to
East Germans, as well as payments for highway improvements or for
the "purchase" of political prisoners—when added in, the amount
exceeded DM 10 billion.[17] Additionally, by the end of 1980 the level of
gross claims of the FRG on the GDR was more than DM 4 billion
(supplier credits, tied bank credits, and trade-related credits, excluding
the swing).

Not only did the GDR benefit in strict financial terms from its
relationship to the FRG, but this relationship allowed it to alleviate
short-term bottlenecks in the economy and to overcome short-term credit
shortages through the use of the swing, which is an interest-free trade
credit line. During the 1970s, the GDR used this credit line extensively.
Inter-German trade has also benefited the GDR in other ways:[18]

- Western technology and urgently needed basic materials and capital
  goods can be acquired.

- The GDR has access to a market for a number of products that
  would be largely closed to it without the favorable policies of the
  FRG, including agricultural products (the result of favorable conditions in the European Community and the nonimposition of the
  value-added tax).

- GDR deliveries to the FRG are mainly in products whose import
  into most other Western countries is subject to broad restrictions;
  inter-German trade is not subject to tariff assessment for the vast
  majority of products.

- The proximity of West Berlin allows the GDR to export goods that are otherwise infeasible because of their high transport costs—about one-third of GDR exports "to the FRG" go to West Berlin.

- The GDR obtained a cost advantage in trading with the FRG because of a common language, easy serviceability, advertising, and so on.

Thus, during the 1970s, the GDR took advantage of its relationship with West Germany and, to a certain degree, became quite dependent on the continuation of this relationship. Particularly when the two oil price shocks hit and the West underwent sharp price increases, the GDR began to depend more heavily on West Germany to alleviate its economic problems. Because of the way energy costs are calculated in the USSR, the GDR did not feel the effects of the first oil price hike until a few years later when the economy began to falter.[19] At this point, the GDR used its ties to Bonn to keep the economy moving and to keep domestic consumption on track through trade, credits, and other projects. East Germany's relationship with West Germany increased its access to foreign capital markets, and it began to borrow heavily in the international capital markets.

The GDR also found that there was a price to pay for its dependence on West Germany. During the 1970s, Bonn was able to use positive linkage to exact political concessions from East Berlin. Bonn linked the extension and increase in swing credit during 1974 negotiations with the East Germans to lower minimum exchange requirements, exclusion of pensions from exchange money, and facilities for the use of private cars for West Berliners and West Germans.[20] But as the 1980s approached, the GDR began to feel that its economic dependence might have grown too much and heightened Bonn's ability to use political blackmail.

The 1980s

After the invasion of Afghanistan and the imposition of martial law in Poland, superpower relations began to deteriorate. At this point, the GDR, which always tried to divorce its economic relations with the FRG from politics, realized that its economy and political stability were vulnerable to changes in superpower relations through its ties to Bonn. Although East Germany benefited from its relationship with the FRG in the 1970s, it became increasingly aware that it could also be damaged by a cooling down of inter-German détente.[21] Thus, the country undertook a two-prong strategy of damage limitation by maintaining an island of détente between the two Germanys and curtailing its economic dependence on West Germany.

East Germany's attempts to keep the lines of communication open between the two Germanys has been analyzed elsewhere.[22] But also important is how the GDR has diversified its international economic relations.

Until 1980, the GDR usually ran a trade deficit with the FRG, which was covered by the swing credit. But since 1980, the GDR has made an effort to keep that account basically in balance. In fact, inter-German trade did not grow significantly during the 1980s, and in 1981 the GDR had a positive account of VE 220.7 million as well as a surplus in 1984. (*Verrechnungseinheiten*, or VE, is adjustment units, the method of payment in East-West German trade.) In the last two years, GDR trade with West Germany has actually declined in real terms. The GDR has also been using less than its full swing credit in the 1980s—thus, despite the decrease in the swing, it does not seem to be affecting the East German economy.

A concerted effort on the part of the GDR to increase its trade with third countries has gone hand in hand with a decrease in the use of inter-German trade.[23] In the 1980s, GDR trade with other industrialized countries increased faster than inter-German trade.[24] From 1982 to 1985, this trade grew at an annual rate of more than 10 percent and was in surplus all three years. "After West Germany, the GDR's largest trade partners in terms of trade turnover have been Austria, Belgium and Luxembourg, France, Britain, Switzerland and Lichtenstein, followed closely by Japan whose exports of capital goods to the GDR more than doubled in 1983."[25]

In addition to diversifying its trade, the GDR consolidated its debt. This was done in part through a decrease in imports and an increase in exports and through domestic austerity. East German net debt with Western countries dropped from $7.78 billion in 1980 to $3.4 billion by June 1985 (excluding inter-German debt).[26] Much of the decrease in GDR debt also came from its increased hard-currency reserves, which were obtained through new longer-term loans. The GDR secured a total of five untied loans in the second half of 1984 on the Eurocredit market, not including the two loans from the FRG. By the beginning of 1985, the GDR had hard-currency reserves of more than $4.2 billion. (That the East Berlin government has not used this to repay most of its outstanding debt implies that it is using this cushion for other purposes—one of which could be to decrease dependence on West Germany.)

In terms of the general state of the GDR economy, the country continued to have positive growth in net material product throughout the 1980s. In 1984 and 1985, per annum growth in net material product was 5.4 percent and 4.6 percent respectively. This impressive growth came on top of average growth rates of 4.5 percent, despite the drop to 2.6 percent in 1982.[27] Thus, although the GDR has tried to diversify its trade away from West Germany and increase its economic ties with other industrialized countries, this does not seem to have had a negative effect on economic growth. Whether the country will be able to continue growing at such a rapid pace is open to debate.

The foregoing analysis does not suggest that the GDR is no longer dependent upon the FRG economically. It does show, however, that the degree of dependence has probably decreased during the 1980s. The GDR's increased trade with other industrialized countries, its increasing use of third-market cooperation agreements,[28] and its healthy hard-currency reserves do point to the fact that the GDR now has a larger cushion than it had in the 1970s. This economic situation allows the East Berlin government more room to maneuver in its dealings with Bonn and limits the ability of Bonn to use economic linkage policies, both positive and negative. As we shall see in the next section, the GDR has been able to stave off attempts by Bonn to use linkage policies and has exacted a higher price for its political concessions to the FRG.

Inter-German Negotiations in the 1980s

The worsening of superpower relations at the end of the 1970s would have led most inter-German experts to assume that relations between the two Germanys would also take a turn for the worst. The two most interesting developments of the early 1980s in inter-German relations were: (1) despite a "second cold war," inter-German relations flourished, and (2) the GDR took the initiative or was the stronger bargaining partner in inter-German negotiations. For our purposes, an examination of the changes in inter-German negotiations is of longer-term importance, although both aspects are linked.

The GDR has come to value its relationship with the FRG and does not seem to worry about West German "contamination" of the "socialist order" or about its undermining East German legitimacy as it once did. Indeed, FRG negotiations with the GDR on equal footing adds legitimacy to the GDR. Moreover, Honecker's *Westpolitik*, apparently undertaken at times against Soviet wishes, is perceived quite positively by East German citizens. Although it is difficult to separate out the various phases of inter-German relations, because they are frequently linked and overlapping, four major negotiations or phases will illustrate the change in inter-German negotiations.

- 1980–1981: the Polish crisis and the increase in the minimum exchange requirement; Honecker's Gera speech and the Honecker-Schmidt meeting

- 1982–1983: the renegotiation of the swing; the *Wende* in Bonn—a new *Deutschlandpolitik* with no strings attached?

- 1984–1985: increasing dialogue despite Soviet objections—more credit, more agreements

- 1985–1986: the refugee problem, with the GDR holding all the cards

1980–1981

With the deterioration of the situation in Poland, the GDR government became increasingly concerned with its ties to West Germany. Its outward criticisms of West Germany and its increasing return to the policies of demarcation were probably equally induced, however, by Moscow's demands. On October 9, 1980, less than a week after Helmut Schmidt's reelection in the FRG, the East Germans announced an increase in the minimum exchange requirement (the entrance fee for West German visitors), from DM 13 to DM 25 and abolished its prior exemption for children less than fifteen years of age and senior citizens.[29] If the goal of this policy was to limit the number of West German, particularly West Berlin, visitors, it was successful. The number of daily visits from West Berlin to the GDR declined by 50 percent within a year; but on the other hand, the GDR did not take in any less hard currency. The Schmidt government threatened retaliation and argued that it went against the spirit of the Four-Power Agreement and the 1974 Swing Credit Agreement.

To add insult to injury, four days later General Secretary Honecker gave a speech in Gera in which he outlined his country's requirements for the continuation of inter-German détente.[30] This was the first time in years that the GDR had raised them so forcefully: full recognition of GDR citizenship; resolution of the Elbe border dispute; establishment of embassies; and dismantlement of the Salzgitter "human rights violations" monitoring center.

The West Germans were at a loss about how to reverse these developments. They marked the lowest point in inter-German affairs since the signing of the Basic Treaty. At first, Hans-Dietrich Genscher tried to apply the strategy that had worked in 1974 to reverse the new exchange requirements—he threatened to lower the amount of swing credits available to the GDR. But this time the strategy backfired. The GDR response was to threaten a cutback in the volume of bilateral trade. Given that trade seemed to be the one untouched area in this new cooling of relations, the FRG backed down.[31]

Through the winter of 1980–1981, inter-German relations seemed to be at an impasse. But by the summer of 1981, things began to improve.

Eric Honecker no longer referred to his Gera demands. Interestingly, the inter-German thaw continued despite the first direct election of National Assembly delegates from East Berlin in June 1981. This action violated Western interpretations of the Berlin Agreement.[32] Moreover, the West Germans did not protest strenuously against this move—something that would have been inconceivable even five years earlier.

By the fall of 1981, despite continuing problems in Poland and the escalation of superpower tensions over the pending deployment of intermediate-range nuclear forces (INFs) in Western Europe, the East and West Germans began to increase their contact. By December 1981, Honecker and Schmidt had finally met in Werbellinsee (after numerous postponements).[33] This meeting was significant for a number of reasons. Not only did it occur during the height of the Polish crisis and martial law was declared during the three-day meeting; it was also the first high-level German-German meeting after the signing of the Basic Treaty on German soil. Most importantly, it showed the first signs that the West German bargaining position was weakening.

As a result of the Werbellinsee meeting, the GDR obtained three concessions from Schmidt without giving anything in return. First, Honecker was able to get an extension on the deadline for renegotiation of the swing, which was to expire at the end of December, until June 1982. Second, "although Schmidt stopped well short of giving into Honecker's [Gera] demands, he did expressly emphasize, quite to Honecker's satisfaction, the GDR's 'sovereignty and statehood.'"[34] Third, the institute that had administered inter-German trade since the end of the war was to be renamed Die Treuhandstelle rather than Die Treuhandstelle für den Interzonenhandel. This gesture furthered GDR claims that the "special" relationship to Germany was based on trade between two sovereign states.

Part of the reason for Bonn's interest in these negotiations was the precarious situation at home. Schmidt was already feeling pressure about the FRG decision to station Pershing II and cruise missiles on German soil. In order to quell domestic opposition, Schmidt had to show some progress on inter-German relations. Additionally, the GDR seemed to be in a better position economically to deal with the FRG. It did not seem to be threatened by a curtailing of the swing, despite its declining international liquidity. In fact, the GDR had not used the full swing credit in 1980 or 1981.[35]

1982–1983

In the next two years, inter-German relations took a couple of surprising turns. The renegotiation of the swing occurred under conditions quite contrary to the expectations of the Schmidt government. The fall of the Schmidt government also showed that even conservative West German politicians could not afford to curtail inter-German relations. They, in fact, went to great lengths to prove their commitment to *Deutschlandpolitik.*

The renegotiation of the swing was finalized on June 18, 1982—weeks before the expiration of the old agreement.[36] The FRG felt that on economic grounds its bargaining position vis-à-vis East Berlin would be strong. At the beginning of 1982, it became clear that the East German economy was running into difficulties. Access to international capital markets was for all intents and purposes closed to the GDR, as its international debt bloomed—40 percent of this debt repayment fell due in 1982 and 1983. Coupled with the financial difficulties of other East European countries, its creditworthiness declined. Thus, the FRG had good reason to believe that it would be able to gain concessions from the GDR on its minimum exchange requirement policy for a continuation of the present swing arrangement.

The political and humanitarian requirements that Bonn placed on the continuation of the swing were, however, unacceptable to the GDR.[37] Instead of giving into these requirements, the Honecker government agreed to a lowering of the swing beginning January 1, 1983. It was to be reduced each year until it reached VE 600 million in 1985. In reality, these reductions would not hurt the GDR economy. In 1982, the GDR only used VE 582 million, less than the 1985 ceiling.

In return, the GDR agreed to a number of quite minor concessions. Daily visits were to be extended from midnight to 2 A.M., and individuals would no longer be prosecuted in GDR courts who illegally left the country before the end of 1980. East Berlin also agreed to open another crossing point for West Berliners traveling to East Berlin. But the GDR did not change its policy concerning the minimum exchange requirement, the one concession that was most vital to the FRG. The GDR clearly came out the winner in these negotiations. Conservative circles accused the government of giving away something for nothing—which perhaps was an accurate assessment of the outcome.[38]

When the Schmidt government fell on October 1, 1982, East Berlin began to worry that the new government would be a harder negotiating partner.[39] Their worries soon proved to be unfounded. Upon taking office, Kohl reiterated the FRG's commitment to inter-German detente, although he threw the word "reunification" around more freely than his predecessors had. For the next six months, there were very few developments in inter-German affairs. This was probably due, in part, to superpower tensions (the deadline for the stationing of INF missiles in the FRG was approaching) and a wait-and-see attitude on the part of both sides. It was probably also due to the transitional nature of the new government—new elections were to be held in March 1983. "Once in office, Kohl continued all ongoing inter-German negotiations and even developed new initiatives. One of his first official acts was the opening of the Berlin-Hamburg highway that had been financed mainly with West German capital. In a series of meetings between high-level East and West German officials new areas of economic cooperation were discussed."[40] Discussions on numerous other areas, including culture and transit, were also conducted in mid-1983.

Franz-Josef Strauss, one of the most conservative politicians in Germany, also went out of his way to prove his commitment to inter-German détente. Although most West German observers argue that this was done more for internal consumption (Strauss was hoping to gain a high profile in FRG foreign policymaking after losing the post of foreign minister to Genscher), it was nevertheless quite unusual. Through negotiations coordinated by Strauss, the GDR was able to obtain a DM 1 billion consortium credit signed on June 29, 1983, guaranteed by the FRG.[41] This loan had no strings attached, was not tied to any specific project, and was the first non-trade-related credit given to the GDR. But if we do look closer at the events around June 29, it does seem that the GDR gave some concessions to the FRG in return for this loan. In September, the GDR abolished its minimum exchange requirement for children less than the age of fifteen and removed some of the automatic firing devices on the border. It is significant that the GDR relaxed some of its prior regulations concerning the movement of individuals across the German border, but these concessions were really quite limited and did not seem to have had a major effect on the GDR.

By the end of 1983, inter-German détente had weathered four years of turbulence. From the crisis in Poland, the change of government in Bonn, to the Bundestag vote to go ahead with the deployment of cruise and Pershing missiles, inter-German relations prospered, despite minor setbacks. During this period, it became clear to the Honecker regime that Bonn was committed to its *Deutschlandpolitik*. A consensus in the country had developed regarding the merits of this policy. Thus, Bonn no longer had one of its major negotiating cards—to walk away from inter-German relations if the East was not forthcoming in negotiating humanitarian concessions. This alone put the FRG at a disadvantage in dealing with the East Germans. In the next three years, Honecker's regime would be able to use this new situation to its advantage and extract further concessions from Bonn.

1984–1985

The year 1984 was of great interest for those concerned with the Eastern bloc because an open rift occurred between the Kremlin and

East Berlin regarding Honecker's *Westpolitik*. The Soviets were clearly displeased about the speed with which inter-German relations were moving forward.

In the first half of 1984, the GDR seemed to make a large concession to the West. The GDR government allowed 31,352 East Germans to resettle in West Germany, a much larger number than had ever been officially sanctioned by the government.[42] Whether this was done to satisfy the West or domestic internal needs remains open to debate. One reason given for this swift change in policy was that the East Berlin government wanted to get rid of many of its "undesirable citizens." Once they were removed, the GDR's emigration policy was again tightened (in May). Additional developments in the first half of the year were agreement on the overground railroad in Berlin and a DM 600 million transaction with Volkswagen.

But more importantly, a second large government-guaranteed credit was announced on July 25, 1984. Like the deal of a year earlier, this one had no explicit strings attached and was not trade related. Additionally, the GDR announced a few minor changes in its border policies. They were:

- Lowering the minimum exchange requirement for pensioners from DM 25 to DM 15

- Extending one-day visas to twenty-four hours

- Increasing the number of days West Germans could spend in the GDR each year from thirty to forty-five (for pensioners, from thirty to sixty)

- Loosening restrictions on "urgent" visits to the FRG

- Improving travel opportunities in the border areas

- Easing regulations on the kind of newspapers and magazines that could be brought into the country from the FRG

- Dismantling the automatic firing devices on the border[43]

Although these concessions seem significant on the face of it, most are only minor changes in existing policy. The final four are open to interpretation, and the last concession had already been promised to the FRG. Moreover, one of the unstated reasons for the credit was to use it as a sweetener for the pending Honecker visit to West Germany in September 1984. The Kohl government had been eager for this visit to occur, partly to show its commitment and progress in inter-German relations. On September 4, the GDR announced that it would have to postpone Honecker's planned visit indefinitely. This was a severe blow to the Kohl government and to its prestige. Through the end of the year, talks continued between the two sides, but it was clear that little would be accomplished for the remainder of 1984.

After the cancellation of his trip, Honecker seemed to change his tactics with regard to West Germany. After being reined in by the Soviet Union, Honecker began a new foreign policy initiative. He shifted his *Westpolitik* to other countries. "Rather than seeking, as before, international acceptance through recognition by the FRG, he openly cultivated relations with Bonn's key political allies in order to put pressure on the FRG."[44] This move served two purposes. First, it increased the GDR's international prestige. Second, it showed the FRG that the GDR was not wholly dependent upon Bonn for international legitimacy and access to other countries, politically and economically.

After a lull in relations, in March, at Konstantin Chernenko's funeral, Kohl and Honecker met with one another and reconfirmed their commitment to the improvement of inter-German relations. It was the first high-level contact between the two governments since the postponement of Honecker's trip.

1985–1986

By the summer of 1985, inter-German relations seemed to be back on track. More importantly, the FRG agreed to increase the swing credit back up to its high point of VE 850 million. This agreement was made in conjunction with a few GDR concessions. It also signaled the beginning of a long debate in the FRG about the problem of political refugees. Of less importance were accompanying agreements on structural improvements in inter-German trade (which benefited the GDR), energy deliveries, and noncommercial payments by the GDR—all minor technical difficulties.[45]

More importantly, the GDR and the FRG ironed out an agreement on the flood of refugees from Sri Lanka who were coming to the GDR (via Interflug Airlines) and crossing the border into West Berlin to apply for political asylum. This problem became a domestic bombshell for the FRG. The refugees could enter the FRG without visa permits because the FRG did not consider the borders of West Berlin to be national borders; therefore they were not controlled as national borders would be.

Finally, the GDR agreed to stem the flood of Sri Lankans into the GDR by requiring them to have a transit visa for the FRG or other West European countries before they were allowed to board Interflug bound for the GDR. The one crucial exception is West Berlin, which the GDR does not consider part of the FRG. Thus, Sri Lankans can still travel to West Berlin, via the GDR, and apply for political asylum and be protected under the West German constitution.[46] Despite the seeming concessions that the GDR made to Bonn in return for trade concessions, the exclusion of West Berlin decreased the significance of this agreement. The East Berliners were able to dictate the terms of the latest round of agreements between the two sides, without giving up much in return. The FRG had a lot more at stake in the conclusion of an agreement on refugees than did the GDR. Furthermore, at the time, the GDR did not seem to need the extra trade credits, given its increased borrowing in the international capital markets and the two FRG-guaranteed loans.

In 1986, when the number of Sri Lankans entering the FRG decreased, the number of political refugees from other countries increased. As before, most of them went to West Germany through the GDR and West Berlin. The number of refugees increased so rapidly that the West Berlin government became increasingly unable to handle the number of cases and house all of the new applicants.[47] A crisis in the country ensued, as many politicians publicly began to wonder if the German constitution were too lenient in this regard. Editorials in conservative as well as other newspapers began to speak of the contamination of the German race and the need for Germany to once again be one race.[48]

The level of hysteria about this issue worried many, but they were at a loss about how to resolve the problem. The Bonn government was at the mercy of the GDR. Bonn could solve this problem only by controlling its borders, changing the Basic Law, or reaching an agreement with the GDR. The first two options would have been political suicide for the government. The third seemed out of its grasp. The FRG tried to appeal to the GDR and entice Honecker's government with economic carrots and sticks. Economics minister Martin Bangemann even warned Honecker that if the flood of refugees did not stop, xenophobia would grow again, which would not be in the interest of either Germany.[49]

The GDR did not seem overly concerned about this problem. It was making money from the arrangement. When the agreement was reached regarding the refugee problem, it was not the ruling coalition government that did the negotiating in September 1986. In fact, it seemed to be unaware that negotiations were going on in East Berlin about the issue. The East Germans reached an agreement with Egon Bahr, long-time innovator and negotiator in inter-German relations for the Social Democratic Party (SPD). This was clearly not a coincidence but a thought-out move. It made the Christian Democratic Union, the Christian Social Union, and the Free Democratic Party look bad domestically. Despite this, the Bonn government promised a number of concessions in return:

- Signing of the Environmental Protection Agreement

- Electronic switching equipment for medical instruments for East Berlin's Charite Hospital

- Signing of a scientific and technical cooperation agreement

- Preferential treatment in trade

The FRG also talked of two other special projects: DM 300 million for desulferization equipment for brown coal electrical utility plants in the GDR; and DM 150–180 million for a road link from the Hamburg highway to Schwerin.

In addition to the clear change in power in this latest round of negotiations, the refugee issue has an ironic twist to it. In the early years after World War II until the construction of the Berlin Wall, the position of West Berlin in the middle of the GDR and its open borders were continual problems for the stability of the GDR. Now the GDR has used these same conditions to its advantage in extracting concessions from the FRG. This twist in the fortunes of the two sides marks, perhaps, the turning point in inter-German relations. The FRG is no longer the stronger partner. It is also fitting that West Berlin would be the site of the latest round of inter-German controversy because it has always symbolized the partition of the two countries and their fragile relationship.

Conclusion

There has been a gradual but significant change in inter-German relations. The East German economy seems to be strong, although problems continue, and some analysts think that the economy will take a sharp downturn before the end of the decade. Nevertheless, the GDR has widened its international economic ties with other Western countries. This has allowed it to decrease its economic dependence on the FRG. Coupled with its broader international economic position is an increasing presence in the political arena. Honecker has met with numerous leaders of Western countries in the 1980s—far more than in any other period of GDR foreign policy history. This has increased the prestige of the East Berlin government at home and abroad. It also seems that despite the 1984 dispute with the Kremlin, the Soviets have given Honecker more room to maneuver domestically and with regard to his *Westpolitik*.

The increased security and legitimacy of the GDR have changed inter-German relations. The GDR does not seem to fear FRG reprisals nearly as much as it did in the past, nor does it seem overly concerned about Western influence. Of equal importance in the change of bargaining power between the two sides is the West German consensus about its *Deutschlandpolitik.* The FRG needs good inter-German relations as much or more than East Berlin does and is willing to make numerous concessions to keep them on track.

The political economy of inter-German negotiations and agreements has thereby changed. The FRG is no longer successful in applying negative linkage to extract concessions.[50] Its ability to use positive linkage has also diminished. In the 1980s, the FRG had to give more in return for smaller concessions on the part of the GDR. Although it is true that both sides have a common interest in keeping inter-German détente alive, the West German interest may be greater. At the same time, negotiations with the GDR have become more costly for the Bonn government. Whether Bonn will be able to continue paying this high price is unclear, but it is clear that the GDR has had the upper hand in the last few years and may continue to possess it in the near future.

Notes

1. See, for example, Wilhelm Bruns, *Deutsch-deutsche Beziehungen* (Opladen: Leske Verlag & Budrich GmbH, 1982); C. Bradley Scharf, *Politics and Change in Eastern Germany: An Evaluation of Socialist Democracy* (Boulder, Colo.: Westview Press, 1984); Arthur Stahnke, "The Economic Dimensions and Political Context of FRG-GDR Trade," in *Joint Economic Committee, East European Assessment,* Part 1, 97th Cong., 1st Sess., pp. 340–375.

2. P. Juling, "Kontinuität im Zeil—aber Wandel des Weges," *Deutschland Archiv* 16, no. 9 (September 1983), p. 925.

3. In the early years of this relationship (until 1975), the GDR did fear that an expansion of inter-German relations could be quite destabilizing for the country. For a thorough analysis of this point see, in particular, James McAdams, *East Germany and Detente: Building Authority After the Wall* (New York: Cambridge University Press, 1985), pp. 68–146.

4. Walter Leisler Keip, "The New Deutschlandpolitik," *Foreign Affairs* 63, no. 2 (Winter 1984-1985), p. 316.

5. These impressions were gained through discussions with Stefan Goebbel of the FRG Permanent Representation and personal contacts with citizens of the GDR in December 1984.

6. For a thorough treatment of this dispute, see Ronald Asmus, "Pravda Attacks East-West German Ties," *RFE/BAD—Background Report* (RFE/BAD)/145, (August 8, 1984); Ronald Asmus, "Pravda Attacks Inter-German Relations Once Again," *RFE/BAD*/151 (August 21, 1984); Ronald Asmus, "East Berlin and Moscow: The Documentation of a Dispute," *RFE/BAD*/158 (August 25, 1984).

7. James McAdams, "Inter-German Detente: A New Balance," *Foreign Affairs* 65, no. 1 (Fall 1986), p. 142.

8. Timothy Garten Ash, "Which Way Will Germany Go?" *New York Review of Books* (January 31, 1985), p. 39.

9. Stephen F. Frowen, "The Economy of the German Democratic Republic," in David Childs, ed., *Honecker's Germany* (Boston: Allen & Unwin, 1985), p. 32.

10. Horst Lambrecht, "The Development of Economic Relations with the FRG," in E. Schulz et al., *GDR Foreign Policy* (Armonk, N.Y.: M.E. Sharpe, 1982), pp. 322 and 340.

11. Paul Gregory and Gert Leptin, "Similar Societies Under Differing Economic Systems: The Case of the Two Germanies," *Soviet Studies* 29, no. 4 (October 1977), pp. 525–526.

12. For a full accounting of Soviet subsidization, see M. Marrese and J. Vanous, *Soviet Subsidization of Trade with Eastern Europe* (Berkeley: University of California, ISS, 1983); Valerie Bunce, "The Empire Strikes Back: The Evolution of the Eastern Bloc from a Soviet Asset to a Soviet Liability," *International Organization* 39, no. 1 (Winter 1985-1986), pp. 1–46.

13. Irwin Collier, Jr., "The GDR Five-Year Plan 1986–1990," in Irwin Collier, Jr., ed., *Workshop on the GDR Economy—Proceedings* (Baltimore, Md.: American Institute for Contemporary German Studies, Johns Hopkins University, May 16, 1986), p. 55.

14. Thomas Baylis, "Explaining the GDR's Economic Strategy," *International Organization* 40, no. 2 (Spring 1986), pp. 390–391.

15. Ibid.

16. Angela Stent, "Soviet Policy Toward the German Democratic Republic," in Sarah M. Terry, ed., *Soviet Policy in Eastern Europe* (New Haven, Conn.: Yale University Press, 1984), p. 53.

17. Gerhard Wettig, "Relations Between the Two German States," in Klaus von Beyme and Hartmut Zimmerman, eds., *Policymaking in the German Democratic Republic* (Aldershot, England: Gower, 1984), p. 295.

18. Lambrecht, "The Development of Economic Relations," pp. 331–332; Frowen, "The Economy of the German Democratic Republic," p. 45.

19. Hanns-Dieter Jacobsen, "Strategy and Focal Points of GDR Foreign Trade Relations," in Schultz, *GDR Foreign Policy*, pp. 147–148.

20. Lambrecht, "The Development of Economic Relations," pp. 310–311.

21. Horst Lambrecht, "Der innerdeutsche Handel—ein Güteraustausch im Spannungsfeld von Politik und Wirtschaft," *Aus Politik und Zeit Geschichte* B40/82 (October 9, 1982), p. 12.

22. In particular, see work done by James McAdams.

23. Raimund Deitz, "Der Westhandel der DDR," *Deutschland Archiv* 18, no. 3 (March 1985), pp. 294–304; Maria Haendcke-Hoppe, "Konsolidierung in der DDR Aussenwirtschaft," *Deutschland Archiv* 17, no. 10 (October 1984), pp. 1060–1068.

24. Jan Vanous, "The GDR Within CMEA," in Collier, *Workshop*, p. 5.

25. B. V. Flow, "German Democratic Republic," in "Economic Ties with the West: How Important Are They for Eastern Europe?" *RFE/RAD—Background Report*/189 (October 12, 1984), p. 12.

26. Haendcke-Hoppe, "Konsolidierung in der DDR Wirtschaft," p. 1067.

27. Collier, *Workshop*, p. 55.

28. Third-market cooperation agreements between the GDR and other Western countries has grown in the 1970s and 1980s. Interestingly, none of these

arrangements has been undertaken with West German firms. See Hannsjoerg F. Buck, "Erhöhung der Aussenhandelseffizienz der DDR durch Unternehmenskooperation zwischen Ost und West?" *Deutschland Archiv* 13, no. 5 (May 1980), pp. 490–509; Sibyle Busch, Karl-Hermann Fink, and Richard Mikton, *Industrial Cooperation Between East and West in Third Countries* (Köln: Bundesverband der Deutschen Industrie, October 1982), pp. 25–32. Compensation trade has also increased during this period, much of which has not been undertaken by West German firms. It averages about $300 million per year. See John Parsons, "Forms of GDR Economic Cooperation with the Nonsocialist World," in Collier, *Workshop*, pp. 9–24.

29. Bruns, *Deutsch-deutsche Beziehungen*, pp. 108–110; Erich Fastenrath, "Erhöhung des Zwangsumtausches und verträgliche Bindungen," *Deutschland Archiv* 14, no. 1 (January 1981), pp. 44–49.

30. Bruns, ibid., pp. 111–114.

31. It should also be noted here that like all *Osthandel*, there are strong domestic economic constituents who would have put pressure on the Bonn government if inter-German trade was threatened. More than six hundred small and medium-sized firms do business with the GDR, and some are quite dependent on this trade. The way that these business interests are organized in Germany makes them a very strong lobbying organization. (This information was gained from personal contact with the interest groups that represent *Osthandel* business interests through the Federation of German Industry in 1985.)

32. Scharf, *Politics and Change*, p. 186.

33. For a discussion of this meeting, see Bruns, *Deutsch-deutsche Beziehungen*, pp. 119–130; McAdams, *East Germany and Detente*, pp. 179–181.

34. McAdams, ibid., p. 179.

35. In 1981, the GDR used on average VE 676 million of its VE 850 million credit. In 1982, this figure fell further to VE 582 million. From *TSI* (Berlin) (February 1984), pp. 4–40.

36. For a discussion of the negotiations, see Jan Hosch, "Ein Erfolg im Schatten," *Deutschland Archiv* 15, no. 10 (October 1982), pp. 1917–1919; McAdams, *East Germany and Detente*, pp. 183–184; Ronald Asmus, "New Inter-German Agreement on 'Swing' Credit Announced," *RFE/RAD—Background Report/141* (June 28, 1982).

37. Scharf, *Politics and Change*, p. 187; Bernard von Plate, "Deutsch-deutsche Beziehungen und Ost-West Konflikt," *Aus Politik und Zeit Geschichte*, B15/84 (April 14, 1984), p. 37.

38. Ronald Asmus, "New Inter-German Agreement on 'Swing' Credit Announced," *RFE Background Report/141* (June 28, 1982), p. 6.

39. Ronald Asmus, "The GDR and the Change of Government in Bonn," *RFE/RAD—Background Report/214* (October 13, 1982).

40. Eric Frey, "Inter-German Relations and the European Alliance System" (Senior thesis, Princeton University, 1985), p. 64.

41. For further details, see Ilse Spittman, "Die Milliardenkredit," *Deutschland Archiv* 16, no. 8 (1983), pp. 785–788; McAdams, *East Germany and Detente*, pp. 187–188.

5

Has West Germany Surrendered in the Battle Against Unemployment?

Daniel J. Broderick

In 1981, unemployment in the Federal Republic of Germany (FRG) reached 5.5 percent, the highest level since 1954. The ruling coalition government at the time was headed by Social Democratic Party (SPD) leader Helmut Schmidt. By the end of 1982, the unemployment figure had increased to 7.51 percent (representing more than 1.8 million unemployed), the Schmidt coalition government had collapsed, and the newly selected chancellor, Helmut Kohl, was calling for early elections. During the subsequent federal election, fought in part over the rise in unemployment under Chancellor Schmidt, the Christian Democratic Party (CDU) of Helmut Kohl soundly defeated Hans-Jochen Vogel's Social Democrats.

After his first year at the helm of the Bundesrepublik, Kohl saw unemployment rise to 9.1 percent, or 2.26 million people. These figures rose to 9.3 percent in 1985 (2.3 million) and settled at 8.9 percent (2.2 million) in 1986. Prior to the 1987 national election, SPD chancellor-candidate Johannes Rau sought to repeat history by using the unemployment issue and hammering away at Kohl's perceived unwillingness and inability to attack this persistent problem. Despite a virtually identical attack to Kohl's in 1983 and with considerably greater ammunition, Rau was unsuccessful in his bid for the chancellorship. Kohl emerged victorious in the winter election.

Does Kohl's victory signify that the West German populace has come to accept and abide this persistent political problem? The purpose here will be to examine unemployment in the Federal Republic of Germany and to determine if, in fact, it is a politically dead issue. By considering, first, the nature and dimensions of the unemployment problem in West Germany and, then, by reviewing some of the governmental measures

Daniel J. Broderick

TABLE 5.1. Unemployment in the FRG, 1950-1986

Year	Number of Unemployed (millions)	Percentage of Private Work Force	Year	Number of Unemployed (millions)	Percentage of Private Work Force
1950	1.58	10.4	1969	.18	0.8
1951	1.43	9.1	1970	.15	0.7
1952	1.38	8.5	1971	.19	0.8
1953	1.26	7.6	1972	.25	1.1
1954	1.22	7.1	1973	.27	1.2
1955	.93	5.2	1974	.58	2.6
1956	.76	4.2	1975	1.07	4.7
1957	.66	3.5	1976	1.06	4.6
1958	.68	3.6	1977	1.03	4.5
1959	.48	2.5	1978	.99	4.3
1960	.23	1.2	1979	.88	3.8
1961	.18	0.9	1980	.89	3.8
1962	.15	0.7	1981	1.27	5.5
1963	.19	0.9	1982	1.83	7.5
1964	.17	0.8	1983	2.26	9.1
1965	.15	0.7	1984	2.27	9.1
1966	.16	0.7	1985	2.30	9.3
1967	.46	2.1	1986	2.22	8.9
1968	.32	1.5			

Source: Compiled from various publications issued by the Federal Department of Labor and Department of Economics.

previously undertaken to alleviate this problem, it shall be evident that any significant reduction in the number of jobless workers through these measures was unlikely. Although some additional measures outlined herein might alleviate more of the problem, such programs are not likely within the current political environment, and time—not the West German government—offers the only possible solution to the nation's unemployment problem.

The Nature and Dimensions
of the Unemployment Problem

Table 5.1 presents the basic dimensions of the problem within West Germany. These figures show some obvious trends. First there is a slow but inexorable reduction in postwar employment. Currency reform, the billions received through the Marshall Plan, and a cooperative labor-management consensus boosted West Germany's industrial production to 75 percent of prewar levels by 1948. Second, the result of this economic miracle was a booming, almost-continuously expanding West German economy. This fueled domestic demand for German products as well as international demand, which resulted in almost nonexistent jobless percentages in the 1960s and early 1970s.[1] Third, unemployment remained at a rather constant 1 million during the mid-1970s. Finally, the early 1980s witnessed a continual and dramatic rise in unemployment, to a point where there are now consistently more than 2 million registered jobless in the nation,[2] representing approximately 9 percent of the work force.

What caused the initial rise in unemployment to 1 million in 1975 and the even more staggering 2 million eight years later? Moreover, why has this level remained so constant? Both of these questions can be explained in large part, and in rough priority of significance, by the following.

Changed Demographics

Increased Birthrate. Babymaking, although a moribund industry now in West Germany, boomed in the 1950s and 1960s. These children entered the work force by the hundreds of thousands in the late 1970s and 1980s to an economy that had ceased to expand and was simply unable to place them in productive employment. Because the birthrates in West Germany did not begin to decline sharply until 1972, the baby-boom phenomena continued throughout the 1980s (and will continue until approximately 1990), thus adding to the unemployment figures.

Women in the Work Force. Once these baby boomers were well on their way to high school (*Gymnasium*) and college, many mothers joined their daughters in the workplace. West German employers were simply unprepared for this development and noticeably unwilling to adapt to it. Consequently, many women, young and old, commiserated together in the unemployment line.

Foreign Workers. West Germany's active recruitment of foreign workers in the 1960s and 1970s had the short-term effect of filling thousands of undesirable jobs necessary to the smooth functioning of the economic miracle. When many of these workers lost their jobs (primarily through reduced production and industrial automation) in the 1970s, they stayed in the country rather than return to the poverty of their homelands. The current number of foreign workers and their families is approximately 4.7 million (about 7.6 percent of the general population).

TABLE 5.2. Labor Costs in Manufacturing Industries (in DM)

Year	Per Capita Total Labor Cost	Direct Earnings	%	Extra Labor Costs[a]	%
1975	30,243	18,582	61.4	11,661	38.6
1982	48,600	27,500	56.6	21,100	43.4

[a]Extra labor costs include paid holidays, social security contributions paid by employers, sick pay, and pensions.

Source: Compiled from Federal Department of Labor figures.

Global Economic Conditions

The world did not stand still while West Germany worked its economic miracle in the 1950s and 1960s. Japan had one, too. Brazil, China, Korea, Singapore, and Taiwan also joined in as stiff competitors to West German traditional trading rivals from Western Europe and the United States. Many markets for the traditional West German exports of food, steel, and coal were no longer importing by the 1970s.[3] Others abandoned many more expensive West German products and materials for cheaper, primarily Far Eastern supplies.

Initially, the government was able to forestall the effect of this competition by using its budgetary surplus to compensate for the loss of industrial sector jobs through increased "make work" programs. The civil service payroll, for example, was increased more than 25 percent. Once this surplus evaporated, the ruling political parties then opted for deficit spending over higher taxes to pay the salaries of these now gainfully, but governmentally, employed. This highly inflationary policy paid the price in higher interest rates and lower investment. With no growth, the federal treasury was ultimately forced to orphan the ever-burgeoning unemployed.

Reduced Investment

Money used for production is obviously money that is unavailable for investment. West Germany had to spend too much money on production costs in the 1970s and 1980s and had nothing left for investment (Table 5.2). The Federal Republic of Germany was highly dependent on oil imports. Sixty percent of its energy needs had to be imported. In 1972, the nation's bill for imported oil was DM 9.4 billion. The world oil crises of 1973–1974 and 1979–1980 raised this bill to DM 45 billion in 1979 and to DM 71 billion in 1981. These higher energy costs were compounded by the additional retooling costs necessary for West German industry to become more energy efficient. Shrinking investment funds became even more minuscule in the 1970s when labor demanded benefits commensurate with the previous decade's booming surpluses.[4]

Unable to quarry investment funds out of such squeezed profits, West German employers were forced to turn to the capital market for investment and expansion funds. Unfortunately, the extraordinarily high interest rates used by the world's governments to fight inflation made this remedy almost impossible. Without funds, there could be no investment, which translated into no growth,[5] no new jobs for those ousted by automation, and no jobs at all for those thousands entering the work force for the first time.

The reduction in investment was not limited to capital goods. West Germany also guaranteed that the unemployment figures would remain constant by significantly reducing money spent on research and development. Expansion of research and development slowed significantly in the 1970s throughout West Germany. Even as late as 1983, only about 2.8 percent of the nation's gross national product (GNP) was earmarked for research and development.[6]

Automation

Although it is true that the manufacturers of automated technology create additional jobs, it is equally true that users of this new technology lose jobs. In West Germany, there were not enough manufacturers to compensate for the loss of user jobs. Technical innovations of the 1970s, particularly in the widespread use of microprocessors (microchips), enabled West German industrialists to replace part of their expensive work force with energy-efficient, labor-barren machines. This process was slowed somewhat throughout the 1970s and 1980s by labor's considerable joint decisionmaking power, particularly in heavy industries. Nonetheless, considerable automation did occur. More than 5,000 industrial robots were in place in West Germany by 1985, and the nation lost more than 500,000 office and administrative workplaces in the decade between 1975 and 1985.[7]

Inflexible Work Force

There are more than one thousand separate occupations listed by the FRG Labor Department. Virtually every career has a legally mandated certification and apprenticeship requirement. On the plus side, this accounts for high-quality goods and services; on the down side, the restrictions create an inflexible, immovable labor force. When new technologies were defining and redefining job after job in the world economies of the 1970s and 1980s, crossing over (and the desire to cross over) to new careers was not occurring in the FRG. Even today, with more than 2 million unemployed, only 270,000 jobless are enrolled in retraining programs throughout the nation.

This professional intractability coincides with a geographical inflexibility that is almost legendary among West German workers. Many unemployed workers in the north simply did not move to fill unoccupied jobs in southern Germany during the 1970s and 1980s.

Treating the Symptoms— Measures to Combat Unemployment

All of the foregoing factors were evident at the time of the 1983 federal elections. SPD candidate Hans-Jochen Vogel rightly claimed no responsibility for the changed demographics or for world economic conditions. Helmut Kohl's 1983 victory, nonetheless, suggests that many in the populace were not pleased with what the prior government *had* done—deficit financing, expensive "make work" programs, and encouragement of careers without a future.[8] Kohl's mandate was to try something else.

In many respects, he did. A tight money policy brought inflation down to practically nothing.[9] The reduction in deficit spending[10] raised confidence in the deutsche mark, and it in turn buoyed in strength against the world's other currencies. The traditionally positive trade balance continued, with West Germany recording a trade surplus in 1986 of $55 billion.

But the strong West German economy under Chancellor Kohl's stewardship still accentuated that one persistently pessimistic economic indicator—unemployment. The CDU/Free Democratic Party (FDP) coalition government, therefore, instituted and continued a series of federal programs directed at the nation's jobless.[11] During Kohl's first administration, there were more than two hundred separate governmental financial assistance programs, at least eighty of which were primarily directed at alleviating the unemployment problem through targeting either the work force or marketplace. Tables 5.3 and 5.4 outline some of these programs.

What was the effect of this panoply of programs? Overall, not much. Between Kohl's first election to the federal chancellorship in 1983 and his second in 1987, unemployment increased by 1.4 percent. How was that possible?

First, some of the initiative, energy, and money directed at the unemployed was dissipated by administrative overlap and duplication. In North Rhine–Westphalia alone, there were ten separate measures to

TABLE 5.3. Selected Federal and State Employment-assistance Programs for the Work Force[a]

Work-force Component	Program	Program Function
Youth	Work programs	Create temporary private-sector jobs for hard-to-place youth[b]
	Vocational training[c]	Create additional private-sector vocational training positions[b]
	Educational and vocational advisory centers	Create and operate several local centers as well as print and distribute more than seventy-five advisory pamphlets, booklets, and leaflets to assist in finding jobs
Women	Work programs	Create permanent private-sector jobs, particularly in industry[b]
	Vocational training	Create additional private-sector training positions, particularly in industry[b]
Foreign workers	Repatriation programs	Pay and assist foreign workers and families to relocate back to homeland
	Refugee assistance	Give favorable credit to employers who hire refugees
Older workers	Early retirement	Pay subsidies to employers to support early, flexible retirement programs, particularly in heavy industries[d]
	Continuing education	Subsidize employers and individuals in major cities to sponsor and attend seminars on new competitive ideas, technologies, and careers

[a]Because the states sponsored the same array of programs as did the federal government, and because funding was intermixed, no effort has been made to identify by name each federal and state program.

[b]These are paid for by tax-free subsidies or favorable credit to employers.

[c]Vocational training has been regulated by law since 1953. More than 70 percent of the work force undergoes some form of it. By 1986, there were approximately 500,000 training positions and more than 650,000 applicants for such positions.

[d]Early retirement laws permit workers to retire at age fifty-eight (usual retirement is at sixty-five) at 65 percent of last average monthly gross pay. Federal Labor Office compensates employers for 30 percent of retiree's wage if jobless or youth is hired to fill vacant job.

Source: Compiled from various publications issued or provided by the Federal Department of Labor, the Federal Department of Economics, and the Ministry for Economics, Small Business, and Technology in North Rhine-Westphalia.

TABLE 5.4. Selected Federal and State Employment-assistance Programs for the Marketplace[a]

Marketplace Component	Program	Program Function
National economy	EC programs	Enable businesses to participate in economic-assistance programs such as the European Investment Bank, the European Social Fund, the European Fund for Regional Development, and the European Coal and Steel Community
	Encouragement of new industries	Provide low-interest loans, tax incentives, and capital subsidies to cover investment costs of foreign companies seeking to expand or relocate in the FRG
	Enhancement of export markets	Provide subsidies for export advice to small businesses, favorable credit for investment in export-producing industries, credit guarantees, subsidies to participate in foreign trade shows
	Support of investment in new technologies	Provide subsidies, risk capital, tax write-offs, favorable credit for introduction, development, or expanded use of new technologies; additional subsidies for increased R&D[b]
	Encouragement of specific industries	Provide subsidies, tax write-offs, and favorable credit for development or expansion of energy-saving investments, environmental protection projects, or urban renewal measures that increase employment and new markets and attract new businesses
	Infrastructure improvement	Provide support to works programs to build and improve national infrastructure

(TABLE 5.4, continued)

Marketplace Component	Program	Program Function
Regional economies	Relocation assistance	Provide capital subsidies, low-interest loans, and other incentives to companies wishing to expand or relocate in economically depressed regions
	Industrial support	Provide subsidies to certain (heavy) industries to create or secure jobs
	Agricultural support	Provide subsidies to farmers
	Small and medium-sized business[c] support	Provide technical advice, low-interest loans, modernization assistance, interest subsidies, and new credit to overcome liquidity crises
	Alternative works projects	Provide free consultation, investment subsidies, and new credit for advancement of alternative works projects

[a]Because the states sponsored the same array of programs as did the federal government, and because funding was intermixed, no effort has been made to identify by name each federal and state program.

[b]Emphasis here is on industrial electronics and information technology. Unfortunately, most of the technological-assistance programs are not keyed to immediate impact on the labor market; thus, some increase, rather than reduce, unemployment.

[c]These make up the largest percentage of employers. For example, there are 450,000 commercial businesses in North Rhine-Westphalia with less than five hundred employees; these entities employ more than 4 million people. By contrast, the twenty largest industrial concerns in the entire nation employ slightly less than 2 million people.

Source: Compiled from various publications issued or provided by the Federal Department of Labor, the Federal Department of Economics, and the Ministry for Economics, Small Business, and Technology in North Rhine-Westphalia.

combat youth unemployment and sixteen different projects to widen the number of vocational training positions.

Second, the bang for the mark just was not that large. Between 1975 and 1984, the West German Regional Joint Development Program spent DM 25.5 billion but created or secured only 175,000 jobs. This is approximately DM 146,000 per job. Because the average West German industrial worker only earns DM 55,000 each year, these were very expensive jobs.

Third, because the government had a limited supply of money to pay out directly, many of these unemployment programs could not operate effectively unless employers first obtained financing from a bank or savings institution. With interest rates about 6 percent higher in the United States during this period, banks were less than eager to lend to risky small businesses so that they could expand their work forces.[12] Thus, the government consistently doled out more of its limited funds as direct loans than it ever did in loan guarantees, and the private banks just did not loan out money at all.

Fourth, the money that the government did spend was not always used to solve the problems for which it was intended. Siemens, for example, received DM 35 million in government assistance funds from the Federal Ministry for Research and Technology to develop a 1-megabit microchip. Siemens then filled the contract, not by hiring new West German workers, but by simply purchasing a chip from Japanese manufacturers.[13]

Finally, and most significantly, none of the previously mentioned government programs did much to alter the major causes of the unemployment problem: demographics, lack of capital investment, and overall business conditions. Consequently, a significant impact on unemployment remained out of the government's reach throughout the 1970s and 1980s.

Addressing the Real Problems—Prospective Programs

During the federal election campaign in 1986–1987, both Chancellor Kohl and SPD opposition candidate Johannes Rau accepted the same basic philosophy of noninterference with private-sector economic decisions.[14] Such self-imposed restrictions on West German political power seem to be accepted by the vast majority of the nation's voters. The largest labor group in the nation, the Federal German Trade Union (DGB), for example, is also resigned to accelerated growth as the primary solution to the nation's unemployment problems.[15] Growth is, of course, a partial answer. But there are others.

Minimizing Demographically Based Influences

Without influence from any outside source, the nation's climbing birthrate halted and began a sharp decline after 1972. But the effect of this will not be felt in the West German economy until the 1990s. Until then, more and more baby boomers will enter the working world and the unemployment line.

To date, the government has instituted some youth-oriented employment and training programs. Several jurisdictions have also added one year of required schooling. The effect of the latter measure is merely to postpone increases in the jobless figures; the effect of the former has not been particularly significant.

A more positive step was taken when the government changed the Employment Promotion Law to permit firms to hire employees for limited periods of up to eighteen months. An additional step would be to exempt certain occupations from the rigid occupational training and employment regulations. Presently, young people must receive lengthy training in a recognized occupation, and the training and certification must be approved by a local chamber of commerce, by local employers, and by a governmental agency. This system discourages part-time work, seasonal or temporary work, job sharing, and any job mobility or experimentation. Instead, the system effectively locks employees into lifelong careers. Although such a practice makes eminent sense with skilled labor positions—masons, welders, electricians—it is simply unnecessary for most retail or service jobs.

West Germany to date remains one of the only Western economies to have less than one-half of its labor force concentrated in the service sector. The reason is that it is simply too costly and unwieldy to hire part-time, temporary, or seasonal workers. Eliminating the ban on private employment agencies and allowing them to bypass the training and certification process for certain jobs would certainly help boost the temporary employment of many young people. Then, once the demographic curve begins to flatten out and it is easier to find permanent employment, the restrictions on nonprofessional service jobs could be reconstructed.

Similar legal restrictions prevent any significant improvement in the employment of women. By statute, women are barred from certain "heavy" work, from work endangering their health, and from work endangering their morals (including some restrictions on overtime and night work). There are additional special protections for mothers. Legal maternity protections include at least six weeks paid vacation prior to the birth of a child and eight weeks paid leave after a child is born. Mothers may take up to twelve additional months of unpaid leave for child care. Women cannot be dismissed during maternity leave for any reason, and a woman has an absolute right to return to her position up to six months after a child is born.

Obviously, such paternalism protects the mother and family from the vagaries of the marketplace, but it hinders the smooth functioning of an employer's operations. The disruptive effects of such legal restrictions can be minimized in large business concerns or in civil service positions. But West Germany is a nation of small and medium-sized businesses, and the impact of these rules on their operations is enormous. Consequently, most employers simply do not hire women.

One possible answer is to exempt some businesses (again, retail and service employers may be the most appropriate choice) from these restrictions entirely or to incorporate needed flexibility into the labor rules governing women. Just as youth benefit from limited employment, women would also be better served by increased part-time, temporary, and seasonal work. At present, such work is not available, and even where it exists, employers must still grapple with job protection laws.

A second measure that would directly impact women in the job market is an easing of the constraints of the nation's shop closure laws. By requiring that stores be open only a limited number of hours per weekday and Saturday, the nation's lawmakers have doubly diminished a woman's employment prospects. First, there are fewer store hours, fewer shifts, and fewer jobs. Second, those women who could find work are discouraged from doing so, unless they (and their liberated husbands) can do all their shopping and errands for the week in four hours on Saturday.

Accelerating Growth

In 1982, the growth rate of the West German economy was an abysmal −1.0 percent. Since then, the GNP has grown by an average of 2.2 percent each year.[16] The Nurnberger Institute for Employment in West Germany estimates that if the growth rate remains at 2.5 percent per year, the number of jobs in the nation will remain the same, as will the number of unemployed, until the year 2000. As the institute concluded, the economy must grow by at least 3 percent a year to reduce unemployment.[17]

Accelerated growth, however, is not something that can be accomplished by government fiat or political rhetoric. Positive trends, such as the drop in world oil prices and the rise in domestic demand, that caused overly optimistic growth projections were quickly offset by the dramatic rise in the West German exchange rate and the increased competition in the domestic market. The West German government should take a much stronger role in encouraging growth for there to be any positive impact on unemployment.

Increasing the Flow of Investment Funds

Present industrial companies within the West German republic are utilizing almost 90 percent of their capacities. Growth is only possible by widening the economy through the founding of new industries and companies, particularly in new growth fields and regions. Publicly, the government can increase its funding support for areas such as biotechnology as well as the current support programs for industrial electronics and information technology. Privately, industries must be encouraged and supported to market aggressively within the developing world their expertise in areas such as lignite and coal mining, steel and heavy machinery production, and environmental controls for heavy industries. Just as these same businesses must find replacement industries within West Germany, there is a growing need for assistance in these fields throughout the developing world.

The key to fighting unemployment within West Germany's borders, however, is to make it easier for businesses to obtain funds to launch new enterprises or to expand their operations.[18] Lower interest rates and a loosened money supply will help.[19] Other possibilities include:

Additional Tax Reform. Tax reduction will free up additional capital for more investment. Future tax cuts, however, should tip toward corporate tax reform rather than toward individual tax cuts. Currently, the corporate tax rate in West Germany is 59 percent on all retained earnings. Coupled with local taxes, the effective corporate tax rate can rise to 70 percent.

Reformation of the Stock Exchange. One of the most utilized ways within the United States to obtain money is through the stock exchange. Within the West German republic, it is not so easy. Only banks and their representatives are admitted as members of the West German stock exchanges and allowed to trade in officially listed shares. There is no U.S.-style over-the-counter stock market. Consequently, a very few financial institutions within the Bundesrepublik exercise a stranglehold on private investment funds.[20] Some incentives need to be created for more diversified and less risk-averse investors. At the very least, West Germany should repeal the .25 percent turnover tax on securities trades to encourage trading and seek to create an over-the-counter market, where small companies can go to obtain capital without going through a bank.

Increasing Bank Regulation. The other traditional route for obtaining capital is credit. Because most West German corporations are greatly undercapitalized, they must resort to bank credit as the sole source of finance. Banks in the nation, however, exert more influence than that of the normal creditor. Banks manage and negotiate *both* sides of virtually every major credit transaction within the country. Deutsche Bank, for example, West Germany's largest financial institution, holds seats on approximately one hundred forty corporate supervisory boards, including all of the major firms (Daimler-Benz, Volkswagen, Siemens, AEG, Thyssen, Bayer, Nixdorf, and Allianz). In addition, Deutsche Bank acts as the financial adviser to many of these companies. The pressure exerted by banks on industry for rapid profits (and consequent dividends to shareholders), therefore, is enormous. Long-term strategies aimed at improvement in competitiveness and employment policies are simply jettisoned.[21] At the very least, a limit must be put on the size of a bank's holdings as well as on the number of supervisory board seats it can hold (or its holding company can control). Encouragement must also be given for more representation and participation by foreign banks in the West German economy.

Improving the Nation's Business Climate

It is not true that *every* West German willing to take a risk did so and emigrated to the United States. There are still individuals and businesses within the nation's borders ready to take some chances. Unfortunately, the overall business climate discourages risk. An entrepreneurial environment must be fostered within West Germany, particularly now that interest rates on capital markets have fallen and fixed securities are no longer such attractive investments.[22] The Aspen Institute for Humanistic Studies in Berlin has proposed some appropriate measures:

- Increase capital availability by advancing the opportunities for seed capital, venture capital, and bridge financing.

- Encourage a risk-taking mentality. West Germans are traditionally very intolerant of failure. Consequently, the nation's bankruptcy laws are too restrictive. By loosening the bankruptcy laws in a way that debtors or failed entrepreneurs are given at least one more chance at obtaining credit, the nation will cease to encourage risk avoidance, and begin to encourage risk taking.

- Simplify the crazy quilt of European market regulations. Although many large Japanese and U.S. companies have apparently mastered the complex patchwork of regulations, fees, and standards[23] presently in existence within the European Community, these restrictions offer very serious start-up barriers to small and medium-sized businesses and insulate established firms from serious challenge.

- Encourage cooperation between industry and universities. German higher education has a strong academic tradition of pure science. The most immediate result of this educational system is that scientific advancements are pursued without the slightest concern for commercial application. By encouraging contracts between industry and universities, the government can create a proentrepreneurial perspective.

As long as the West German deutsche mark remains so strong, the incentive for business to relocate or expand within the nation (as opposed to Great Britain, Italy, or elsewhere) is exceedingly small. Nonetheless, additional incentives are necessary to improve the business climate so that those firms that are already there will remain and prosper.

Adjusting Social Labor Laws

In contrast to other wage earners throughout the world, workers in West Germany who *are* employed manage very well. The average salary for an employee in an industry with fifty or more employees is about DM 25,000 per year. This base is then enhanced by a number of enviable perqs:

- Each worker receives on average of about DM 30,000 annually in vacation pay, sick pay, bonuses, profit sharing, insurance costs, and training costs. ·

- Each worker receives a minimum of four weeks paid vacation per year, with most receiving about six weeks per year.

- Employees who suffer from some prolonged physical ailment or merely from emotional or psychological stress may add to this vacation by "taking a cure" at any one of the numerous spas or resorts advertised in every daily newspaper.

- Workers in most states can also take advantage of the liberal continuing education laws. In North Rhine–Westphalia that law permits an employee to take off five days with pay per year for continuing education. This education may be training in advanced technologies or new production methods, but it may also involve "political education" concerning rights as a citizen.

- Many employees are required to work only a thirty-eight or thirty-eight and one-half hour work week, with a possibility of that being reduced to a thirty-five-hour work week in the future.

Wage and fringe benefits are only a part of the elaborate social security system. There are labor laws governing the length of work contracts, part-time work, firings, protection of workplaces, early retirement, employment of disabled, employment of women, age discrimination, and continuing education. Even if an employee is laid off, generous employer/employee-funded employment benefits act to reduce the trauma. The nation's jobless receive almost 70 percent of their prior net income for one year, then almost 60 percent for another year, and finally about 30–35 percent thereafter as welfare payments.

Such high labor costs and elaborate legal restrictions served West Germany and West German employees well as long as industry was able to match rising salaries with increased productivity and new markets. When this expansive growth stalled in the 1970s and 1980s, West German employee unions[24] were able to limit staff reductions to natural attrition and early retirement. But the lack of expansion has not allowed employers to absorb any new workers, and these new workers raised West German unemployment from less than 1 million to more than 2 million.

Putting these new workers on the payroll requires some adjustments in labor costs as well as in social labor laws. Otherwise employers will continue to opt for machines over humans and foreign men over West German men and women. A positive start in this direction would be to build into the system some needed flexibility to hire and fire. Presently, it takes about six months to replace or fire a worker, and all dismissals that are socially unjust are null and void. If exemptions for certain part-time, seasonal, or short-term work were constructed, particularly in service fields, employers might not be so adverse to new hires and so in favor of overtime. An even stronger step would be for employees, unions, and workers with jobs to accept less (or merely to accept no more) in return for increased hirings. A return to the forty-hour week, rather than the thirty-five-hour week, would help by freeing up additional funds for investment and growth. But this prospect is as unlikely as any other proposed reduction in West Germany's comfortable social security system.

Conclusion

Chancellor Kohl's reelection in 1987 signifies, perhaps more than anything else, an acceptance by the West German people of their present condition and an unwillingness to tamper with this state. For the most part and for most citizens, West Germany today is in enviable health. Employed workers are enjoying the fruits of four decades of prosperity, spending inflation-free, potent deutsche marks at home and abroad.

Politically, the nation sits in a rather comfortable landscape, devoid of any significantly pernicious domestic or foreign ills.

To the extent that unemployment mars this otherwise rosy picture, the problem has seemed to stabilize, and now hovers at about 9 percent. Even though this translates into 2 million unemployed, the situation has not manifested itself in domestic turmoil, upheaval, or even a change in government.

Thus, the government and West German people seem content to treat the afflicted with social benefits and financial assistance for the time being, while awaiting the cure that time will bring in the next century. Rushing a cure now, although possible, appears unlikely. The ills that this could raise—inflation, deficits, instability, and discontinuity—are among things that the 20 million West German workers who are employed do not seem willing to risk.

Notes

1. Most economists agree that some unemployment is unavoidable and serves to regulate labor supply and wages. Nonetheless, West Germany's jobless rates in the 1960s and 1970s went beyond this level of structural unemployment, and the nation was forced to recruit thousands of foreign workers from the poorer regions of southern Europe.

2. Most observers of the West German scene agree that there are also thousands (up to 1.3 million by one estimate) of unregistered unemployed. These people in the "still reserve" have responded to the depressed labor market either by giving up trying to register and seek work or by never registering in the first place.

3. West Germany exports almost 30 percent of its gross national product. Thirty percent of the domestic labor force depends on export-related jobs.

4. West German citizens pay almost 40 percent of their current income to the state through taxes and social payments (compared to 28 percent and 27 percent in the United States and Japan, respectively). A hefty portion of this money (30 percent of West Germany's GNP) goes to support social insurance programs (old age, health, accident, unemployment), social compensation programs (payments to war veterans, children, renters), and welfare programs (disability, unemployment benefits, vocational training and counseling).

5. The growth of the nation's GNP during this period showed some startlingly bad years. Adjusted for inflation, real growth was .5 percent in 1974; −1.6 percent in 1975; −.2 percent in 1981; and −1.0 percent in 1982.

6. The Japanese, by contrast, spent 9–10 percent of their GNP on research and development in 1970; dropping to 8.4 percent in the 1970s; and dropping again to 5–6 percent in the 1980.

7. The West German corporate giant Siemens has conducted a study predicting that by 1990, 25–30 percent of *all* office workers in the nation will be automated, thus eliminating an additional 1.5 million jobs. Siemens's position as the

manufacturer of much of this technological hardware may slant these projections a bit on the optimistic side, but the trend is certainly correctly noted.

8. In the spirit of true egalitarianism, the SPD encouraged young people to pursue whatever best suited their personal interests and not to limit themselves to realistic, economic possibilities. Consequently, between 1990 and the year 2000, there will be approximately 3 million young academics seeking employment in a market of only 1 million jobs.

9. In 1974, the inflation rate was approximately 7 percent; by 1986, the inflation rate had dropped to -0.2 percent.

10. By 1986, the federal deficit was DM 25 billion, the lowest level since 1977.

11. Johannes Rau, Kohl's opponent in the 1987 federal campaign, has been minister president for North Rhine–Westphalia (NRW) since 1978. It is the most populous state in the Bundesrepublik and the state with the highest number of unemployed. Virtually every federal assistance program instituted or coordinated by the federal government under Kohl has a counterpart in NRW—works programs, subsidies for new businesses, sponsorship of new technology, financial assistance for small and medium-sized businesses, and so on.

12. In 1985, Deutsche Bank had a full operating profit of more than DM 4 billion. During that same year, it reported zero risk provisions.

13. Even today, the Bonn government has given DM 240 million to Siemens to develop a 4-megabit superchip, when Siemens readily admits that 20 percent of any new jobs it creates are in foreign countries.

14. Johannes Rau did support in spirit the unions' demands for a shorter work week. West German workers unions have focused their collective bargaining demands on the issue of a shorter work week, asking in most instances for a thirty-five-hour work week. In the spring of 1987, the Metalworkers Union agreed to a phased-in thirty-seven-hour week.

15. In championing a reduction in the work week to thirty-five hours, the DGB maintains that more than 650,000 new positions will be created by reducing the work week by one hour and that a thirty-five-hour work week would create an additional 1.2–1.3 million jobs. These optimistic projections are based in part upon the thousands of jobs created and secured in the steel industry by the 38-hour week. But this result stemmed largely from the ability of the steel industry to absorb new workers because of a twenty-four-hour-a-day operation; most West German businesses cannot do this. Nonetheless, even the DGB concedes that a thirty-five-hour work week can survive only with accelerated growth.

16. Economic growth in the Bundesrepublik (adjusted for inflation) was 1.3 percent in 1983, 2.6 percent in 1985, and 2.5 percent in 1986.

17. With 3 percent growth, the institute predicted that the reduction in unemployment will be approximately 75,000 per year; with 4 percent growth, the reduction will be 150,000.

18. The 20 million new jobs that have been created in the United States since the mid-1970s resulted almost entirely from the ease with which businesses, particularly small businesses, were able to get money.

19. In December 1987, the West German government announced a $12.7 billion low-cost loan program designed to aid local governments and small businesses. In addition, the West German central bank reduced its discount rate to 2.5 percent, a record low level.

20. West German banks hold unlimited shares of stock in industrial concerns, control portfolios in the billions for investment funds and private investors, and administer shares for the small stockholders that do exist. West German banks hold more than 5 percent of the capital of all joint stock companies (Deutsche Bank alone has a 28.5 percent interest in Daimler-Benz).

21. In 1984 and 1985, virtually all of the twenty largest industrial concerns within West Germany experienced increased sales and profitable years. During that same period, they reduced the number of employees by 1.6 percent, or 35,000 people.

22. It was not until 1983 that investment by entrepreneurs overtook investment in fixed-market securities.

23. Most Japanese electronic equipment marketed in Europe comes fully equipped with adapters fitting every electronic outlet, from Britain, to France, to West Germany. This practice is simply not possible for many small or medium-sized companies.

24. Labor's powerful voice in virtually every management decision affecting labor, wages, and benefits stems primarily from the joint decisionmaking system in place in virtually every large West German industry. This power was wielded extensively in the 1970s and 1980s to reduce or eliminate staff cutbacks.

6

Environmental Conditions for Innovation in the Federal Republic of Germany

David R. Larrimore

Innovation and the process of applying new technology to products or services are subjects of vital concern in the Federal Republic of Germany (FRG). Germany has traditionally played a leading role in innovation, especially in chemical and electrical goods in the late nineteenth and early twentieth centuries and during its Phoenix-like resurrection after World War II, which created the "economic wonder" of the 1950s and 1960s. Media reports regarding innovation and technology in the FRG during the past few years, however, have overflowed with phrases such as "hobbling," "falling behind," "dependent upon other countries for technology," "innovation weakness," and "outdated." A popular anecdote illustrates the current trend:

> In January the Americans announced a new theory. In February the Russians claimed that it had been discovered and patented in Russia 30 years ago. In March the Japanese began producing the first products embodying the theory and offering them for sale. In April the FRG held its first meeting to select a committee and set a date for the committee to begin discussing the innovation, its benefits and risks, and whether it should be adopted in the FRG or not.

Although this scenario does not apply to all areas of the economy— such as the automobile and machine tool industries in which the FRG has maintained, and often improved, its position due to product quality and dependability—it appears to be universally acknowledged that deficits exist in the so-called high technologies. These include electronics and many of its applications (computers, communications), lasers, and biotechnology.[1] This lag in the practical application of new technologies into products and services clearly has a dragging effect on economic growth. Several internal and external studies commissioned by the government of the FRG have shown a positive correlation between technological modernity and firm/industry competitiveness.[2] The results of these studies demonstrated that those industries that adapted to new technologies had a net growth in jobs, whereas those that attempted to protect themselves from change (such as steel and shipbuilding) sustained a net loss of jobs. With the current 2.5 million jobless in the FRG and the corresponding costs to the economic and psychological well-being of the citizenry, it is imperative that the necessary steps be taken to close this gap in technological competitiveness.

Research and Development Expenditures/Project Costs

The study must begin by comparing 1985 expenditures for research and development (R&D) in the FRG, the United States, and Japan. Although the expenditures relative to gross domestic product (GDP) are roughly the same in these countries (2.8 percent for the FRG and United States, 2.6 percent for Japan,) the United States and Japan spent 5 and 1.7 times as much in total R&D expenditures as the FRG did.[3] Expenditures for individual research projects, in terms of both human and capital resources, have grown rapidly in recent years and especially fast in the high technology areas. This limits the ability of the FRG to conduct comprehensive research, however, because if funding is concentrated on individual firms and the domestic market, many large projects will never reach the breakeven point. To be feasible, large projects require an economic setting that offers the requisite production facilities and correspondingly large markets, such as the United States, Japan, or the European Community.

Many large projects have been government-funded in the United States and Japan. The European Community (EC) has participated in a number of similar projects, including Airbus, the European Strategic Program for Research and Development in Information Technologies, the European Space Agency, as well as atomic energy research.[4] More of these transnational projects will be necessary, at the governmental or private industry level, if the FRG and the EC are to catch up and keep pace with worldwide developments in the high technologies.[5]

Not only are large projects such as the foregoing necessary for the commercialization of many technologies; small, fast-reacting companies have also driven the commercialization process in the United States and other countries. This chapter is concerned with large, existing firms and with small, newly created firms as the means to disseminate and apply technology.

West Germany's system has built-in hindrances to the speedy commercial application of new technological discoveries. The causes seem to be rooted in several areas, chief among them:

1. Insufficient incentives for technology commercialization (taxes and tax incentives, strong social net, small markets)

2. A highly structured economy as well as tightly structured, or specialized, business and research organizations

3. Insufficient information "flows" (creation, collection and distribution) among people, institutions, and the country as a whole

4. Insufficient "real" venture capital aimed toward new startups in high-technology areas

5. Reactive financial and market strategies

6. Skepticism toward risk taking, new or small ventures, and individualism

Incentives

In the FRG, there are few economic incentives for an individual to launch a risky venture in hopes of "striking it big."[6] There are high personal and business taxes as well as high social insurance costs to pay. The downside costs are also extremely high due to the employee termination costs associated with a bankruptcy. Additionally, the cost of a bankruptcy can follow an individual for up to thirty years. Most firms are satisfied with a 2 to 6 percent return on investment; this is a very narrow margin for a high-risk start-up. As the chair of a prominent international financial services group has observed, "If an investor subscribes to a life-insurance annuity, he can get a 6 percent return, tax free, in twelve years. If you are silly enough to start a firm and hire people, your margin may equal 2 percent, and your tax rate will be 70 percent."[7]

In contrast to the United States, there are no special investment tax credits or tax write-offs for R&D costs in the FRG. Other R&D-related costs, such as social insurance, are higher in the FRG.[8] Thus, governmental "barriers" to the success of a new venture are more imposing in the FRG than in the United States.

The employee benefit package also works as a disincentive to an entrepreneurial venture. The comfortable thirty-five to forty-hour work week and four to six week vacation must be forsaken. New entrepreneurs are also required by law to grant long vacations to their employees. Wages are quite high in the FRG, and the labor market is illiquid.

The formation of a limited-liability firm is expensive and tightly regulated in the FRG, unlike in the USA. For example, the formation of a GmbH, the German equivalent of a U.S. corporation, costs DM 50,000 (at the current exchange rate, more than $25,000). In the United States, incorporation costs a few hundred dollars.

In sum, the upside potential (profit) is limited, whereas the downside risk (losses) is virtually unlimited. Is it any wonder, then, that most Germans choose a safer, lower-risk route?

Highly Structured Organizations and Economy

Firms in the FRG tend to be highly structured, and their organizational charts provide a very accurate guide to the authority inherent in a given position. Less rigidity obtains in the United States. Many indirect linkages occur, and the organizational chart (with the exception of upper levels of management) often does not provide a good map of the relative positions of authority in the firm.

The economy is also highly structured in the FRG and is a social market economy with "state control where necessary." Thus, the Bundespost controls all means of communications (mail, telephone, microwave, satellite). Services are limited, and other equipment cannot be attached to the government network (a monopoly situation akin to Bell Telephone's former position in the United States). As a result, some multinational enterprises (MNEs) are moving their electronic data processing operations out of Germany.[9] This central control of telecommunications is also a problem for financial trading, particularly in the stock markets. In addition, there are no private mass media broadcast stations.

In the marketplace, prices for a given product are uniform regardless of the size of the seller, which is a result of the Unfair Competition Law. This price uniformity applies to consumer goods not only through the foregoing law but also through the Retail Shop Protection Law. The price of a product is the same whether it is purchased through a large department store or through a small, usually family, business, known in Germany as a Tante Emma shop. Working conditions as well as employee rights and benefits are also tightly regulated by the government and differ little between large and small firms. These rules even extend as far as regulating the hours stores can be open (until 6:30 P.M. on workdays, 2:00 P.M. on Saturdays, 6:30 P.M. on the first Saturday of each month, and never on Sundays), how many sales can be held, and how much of a discount may be offered.

These regulations, in reducing business flexibility, also reduce competitiveness. They also produce a less flexible labor market, both in terms of geographic/functional mobility and wages. With less maneuvering room than one finds in the United States, it becomes difficult for German firms to differentiate themselves.

This higher degree of structure and compartmentalization of businesses in the FRG reduces mobility among functions, business units, and groups. The "team concept" is being applied in some larger firms, but with little success to date because it requires employees to be given the authority to make decisions without higher-level intervention. Most German managers have a difficult time delegating sufficient authority to their subordinates. Thus, consultation among specialists remains the standard mode of development in most aspects of business. In addition to this form of high-level planning, German firms also try to plan their innovations in great detail. This is a self-defeating practice, however, because most innovations, by their very nature, cannot be planned in detail or fit into a neat timetable.

Information Flows

Information flows much less freely in the corporate world of the FRG than in the United States. The "open door" policy often practiced by U.S. high-technology firms is virtually never seen in the FRG. This results from the highly structured nature of German business—information flows along the organizational lines of the individual firms.

Cross-flows of information between organizational levels, functions, and institutions are the exception, rather than the norm. Consequently, there seems to be a low awareness of what other firms, industries, or countries are doing in certain fields of business or technology. Institutional libraries in the FRG tend to have narrower and more limited collections than do similar organizations in the United States. Additionally, few German-language data bases are available in the FRG, and the U.S. data bases are rarely consulted. Thus, work is often unnecessarily duplicated, and documented blind alleys may be thoroughly reresearched. Perhaps the most telling statistic is that the United States has 76 percent (more than 1,800 units) of the world's data banks; the FRG has just 3 percent.[10]

It is also uncommon in the FRG for individuals to move among positions in government, universities, national research institutions, and private firms. Thus, the exchange of experiences is limited, which often leads to an inbreeding of ideas. German institutions may often be unaware of competitors' actions, new breakthroughs in their areas, or improved products or techniques for conducting their work.

The low level of activity by German (especially chemical) firms in biotechnology is particularly striking.[11] The processing technologies are a major bottleneck in the commercialization of biotechnology. German chemical firms excel in process design and yet, to date, have been very cautious in entering this field. Hoechst has been the most aggressive, but the resources committed to this area are still not significant. Recent reports indicate that only four to eight researchers from the German parent have been "loaned" to U.S. universities. All German firms in this field could profit by closer cooperation.

Limited information flow is a most disturbing characteristic of institutions in the FRG. Given the importance of intellectual networking in innovation and the translation of technology to practical application (as practiced in Silicon Valley and in Japan), limited flow is particularly counterproductive. Electronic mail is virtually nonexistent, and very few personal computers are in use, even by managers. Moreover, the German print media, in contrast to their U.S. counterparts, do not report on technology developments in a sufficiently broad and well-balanced manner.

Availability of Capital

German banks control the availability of capital. Because the banks control new bond issues as well as new stock issues, and are also the largest holders of stocks, they have determined who obtains funds and for what purpose. Banks are notoriously conservative institutions, more interested in investing in firms with buildings and equipment, or other "hard" goods, than in higher-risk (but potentially high-payoff) businesses whose assets consist mainly of ideas, or "soft" goods. Through interlocking directorates, many Aufsichtsrat (board of directors) members are cross-connected, particularly because banks own most of the stock. As the banks are also board members in most firms, they have been able to exert influence over investment decisions. Thus, most business firms are also financially conservative (consider Siemens' DM 20 billion liquidity). There is much discussion in the FRG about the "Club of 200," which is reputed to control the economy.

Venture capital (VC) was virtually nonexistent outside the Wagnisfinanzierung Gesellschaft (WFG) until approximately 1983, when the Bundesministerium für Forschung und Technologie (Federal Ministry for Research and Technology), or BMFT, held a convention that spurred the creation of additional VC firms. The BMFT program TOU (a promotional program for new technologically oriented firms) is the only true "risky" venture capital in the FRG.[12] It amounted to DM 60 million in 1985. The VC firms are still too conservative, however, investing most typically in firms that need money to expand facilities, tap new markets, or manufacture finished prototypes.[13] The WFG in particular is very risk averse because it is controlled by the banks and must show a profit. The banks are short term in their financial orientation. Thus, they are not interested in financing a firm that will show losses for some years, which a newly founded, technologically based company is almost certain to incur.

Obtaining funds by going public in the stock market is also difficult in the FRG. Entry requirements are stringent; entrance fees are high; and secondary markets similar to the over-the-counter market in the United States, while recently expanded in the second half of 1986, are still minuscule. Because of the strict entry requirements there are few stocks and even fewer new issues, and banks control the stock markets, own most of the stocks, and conduct all market transactions. There have traditionally been few private investors because there is no insider-trading law and associated government enforcement institution (like the Securities and Exchange Commission in the United States) to protect them. Companies' annual reports offer little useful information with respect to finances or future plans, and little analysis is done for the public because the major stockholders (the banks) have access to all the information they need, either through their board connections or through direct examination of the books in their role as creditors. All stock markets are locally controlled; there is no federal oversight. In this connection, it is interesting to note that no one has ever been prosecuted for manipulating (or attempting to manipulate) the market.

There is also evidence that the German public does not invest in stocks because of its risk-averse attitude; Germans want a return that is certain. As an example, the Ministry of Finance often receives letters and phone calls from small investors who say that they invested in a stock whose price then dropped, and they want to know who in the government is going to pay them the difference. They believe that they should be protected from losses by the government!

Financial and Market Strategies

U.S. firms adopt long-term production and marketing strategies but short-term financial strategies because of intense scrutiny by financial analysts and institutional holders. In the FRG, on the other hand, there is much more long-term financial strategizing (because the banks hold stock for long periods) but short-term strategizing with respect to marketing and production.

Established firms in the FRG generally wait until standards are set and the initial shakeout has occurred before they enter a new market area. They can then concentrate on rationalization of the product and obtain high-efficiency production. The firms thereby lose the "first-mover" effect but also spare themselves the inefficiencies of the initial development and marketing efforts. Once they enter the market, the basic development work is already done, and they can concentrate on application, thus building the most modern facilities in terms of economy of scale and automation.

This was a wise strategy when product and technology life cycles were long and the learning curve was not as steep as it currently is.[14] In present conditions, however, it is a precarious strategy. In many high-technology areas, only the first player to reach the market with a new product or service will make a profit; all the others play at a loss to gain experience and hope to be the first on the market with the next generation.

Societal Attitudes

Virtually all segments of German society will accept lower returns on investments because of the correspondingly lower risk. This characteristic aversion to risk is attributable, at least in part, to Germany's severe bouts of financial instability in the first half of this century, including the inflation that ensued after both world wars and the intervening Great Depression.

Changing careers, functions, or locations in midlife has been almost unthinkable for Germans (although there are indications this rigidity is beginning to soften). The effect of this thinking process is to make the German work force less adaptable to the winds of economic change than are some of its competitors.

The German business community takes a very dim view of entrepreneurial failures. If a new venture does not succeed, a young entrepreneur may never find the financial banking to try again. Ironically, even successful entrepreneurs receive their share of disapproval in society. In the more "socialized" environment of the FRG, an individual who is very successful may be suspected of taking advantage of the rest of society, of having done something immoral or illegal.

On the political front, the FRG government is not very accepting of differing views. For example, just when it thought the Greens would fade into oblivion, their coalition with the Social Democratic Party (SPD) in Hessen (December 1985–February 1987) breathed new life into the party. In Bonn, the ruling coalition reacted with shock, declaring the Greens/SPD coalition to be the worst thing that had happened to Hessen and to the republic. A number of firms, including Hoechst, threatened to invest elsewhere. Newspaper reports foretold "doom and gloom" for Hessen and for Germany because this "disease" would probably spread.

Until recently, unions have been against introduction of new technologies into the workplace. It was feared that they increased specialization of labor and caused the loss of jobs. But unions have discovered that those industry branches that adopted new technology had a net addition of jobs, whereas those that attempted to remain static through public aid or through a rejection of change experienced a net loss of jobs. Nevertheless, unions are still seeking to extend their rights of codetermination in the workplace to cover introduction of new technologies.

New technologies also face the challenge of the skeptical German consumer, who feels at home with his or her older technology and resistant to a new interloper.[15] The German public sometimes seems almost too eager to find fault with new technologies or evidence of their failure, as illustrated by the picture of Silicon Valley painted in the following headlines:

"Chips and Poor Wretches"—*Die Zeit*, September 6, 1985

"Silicon Valley: End of a Myth"—*Computer Magazine*, September 1985

"Clouds Over Silicon Valley"—*Chip*, August 1985

"Silicon Valley—Victim of Its Own Success: High Technology No Guarantee for Jobs"—*Frankfurter Allgemeine Zeitung*, October 14, 1985

"Way of the Smithy or the Demon of Technology: Our Industrial Society Between Security and Fear"—*Die Welt*, July 13, 1985

German consumers also like to purchase goods that have long lifetimes. This phenomenon increases the time required to introduce a new technology into an old product line because the old units continue to be maintained and used and the demand for new units is correspondingly reduced.

Thus, the German attitude toward the introduction of new technologies into society is to resist explosive growth (as experienced by the United States) in the computer industry. The Germans feel it is better to sit, wait the confusion out, and then move in once there is some form and rationale to a market. They ask the question, "Should we adopt this technology?" and attempt to calculate and discuss all of the possible costs and benefits of its usage instead of embracing new technologies and ideas and trying them out with the "How do we adopt it?" attitude found in the United States.

The government, to its credit, has been rather innovative in trying new measures designed to overcome the FRG's deficit in the technology race. The measures include:

1. Providing the spark for venture capital in the FRG by means of the BMFT convention in 1983 as well as government funding through the TOU program

2. Targeting certain technology areas with special funds, such as biotechnology, applications of microelectronics, microperipherals, and new materials (like ceramics and composites)

3. Introducing new proposals to reform taxes, especially the *Gewerbesteuer* (business tax)

4. Introducing proposals (in the second half of 1986) that should make it easier for small firms to "go public" and issue their own stocks

5. Instituting programs to promote transfer of knowledge among universities, national research institutes, and private firms (for example, the Personnel Cost Subsidy Program of the Ministry of Economics and the Young Leading Researchers Program)

6. Participating in pan-European programs, such as the European Strategic Program for Research and Development in Information Technologies and the European Research Coordination Agency (although the current outlook for these programs, particularly the latter, is not especially hopeful)

Other Observations

There are several other points that have not been developed in the context of this chapter but that are worth noting. They are as follows:

1. Joint research—The Federation of Industrial Research Associations (AIF) does applied research for small and midsize firms through its member alliances and institutes. The Fraunhofer Gesellschaft also does applied research. The German Research Society does basic research, as do the national research institutes (such as the Association of National Research Centers). The AIF could provide a rapid way to network within and across industries, as well as spread the costs of precompetitive development among the firms.

2. Protection of technology—Patent laws are the only form of protection, and patents are expensive. There is a high registration fee, and the maintenance costs increase steeply each year. This fee structure is intended to promote the rapid translation of patents into products. Moreover, the problem of industrial espionage from East Germany is very real.

3. Cooperation within the European Community—the FRG, as a nation heavily dependent upon exports, wants a unified market with common equipment standards throughout the community and coordinated taxes. Old rivalries in Europe do not die easily, however, and the diverging national interests of the member states have prevented this ideal from being fully realized. One hopeful development in the past few years has been the increased cooperation of European MNEs. Major agreements have been reached in telecommunications and computer operating systems, and others on software and hardware standards are in the offing.

Conclusion

The FRG certainly has the raw technological talent to conduct excellent basic research. But it has severe failings with respect to the timely translation of basic discoveries into marketable products. Although the United States may be in need of more order (which generally takes place through "rationalization" of markets after heady growth periods), the FRG is definitely in dire need of some added chaos if the seeds of today's innovations, particularly those of the "information society," are to blossom. If the FRG can make the changes it needs to encourage more entrepreneurial activity, it may yet prove a formidable competitor in the fields of high technology.

Notes

1. "Survey, West German Economy: Low on High-Tech," *The Economist* (February 4, 1984), pp. 8–12; E. Heusser, "Zukunftstechnologien and Patentbilanz: Transparente Forschung und Entwicklung," *Blick durch die Wirtschaft* (October 10, 1985), p. 3 ff; and R. Burkhardt, "Innovation in Deutschland: Kampf gegen Patente," *Wirtschaftswoche*, no. 19 (May 4, 1984), pp. 78–94.

2. Prognos AG Basel & Mackintosh Consultants Co., *Technischer Fortschritt Auswirkungen auf Wirtschaft und Arbeitsmarkt* (Basel: Prognos AG, October 1979); and BMWi, *Technologische Entwicklung und Beschäftigung*, Dokumentation no. 268 (Bonn: Prognos AG, July 1985).

3. Battelle-Institut e.V., *Forschungesbudget 1985: Forschung und Entwicklung in der Bundesrepublik Deutschland* (Frankfurt am Main: Battelle-Institut e.V., April 1985).

4. OECD, *Science and Technology Policy Outlook, 1985* (Paris: OECD, 1985).

5. BMFT, "EUREKA soll Europas Wettbewerbsfähigkeit steigern," *BMFT-Journal* (August 1985), p. 3.

6. G. Fischer, "Stange im Nebel," *Manager Magazine* (November 1985), pp. 176–182.

7. H. Heck, "Unternehmenssteuern: Deutsche Firmen werden am stärksten zur Kasse gebeten," *Die Welt*, October 8, 1985, p. 13.

8. L. Fischer, "Die Steuerbelastung der deutschen Unternehmen im internationalen Vergleich," *Wirtschaftsdienst* 1 (1985), pp. 33–41.

9. F. A. Miller and J. Heard, "Multinationals: Fed up with the Bundespost," *Business Week* (International) (November 18, 1985), p. 36.

10. "Datenbanken: Mittelstand im Abseits," *Industriemagazin* (November 1985), pp. 218–222.

11. W. Gehrmann, "Forscher entdecken den Profit: In der Bundesrepublik beginnt der Boom der Biotechnik," *Die Zeit* (September 27, 1985), p. 25.

12. Bundestag, "TOU und Wagniskapital," *Protokoll Nr. 41 des Ausschusses für Forschung und Technologie* (September 11, 1985), pp. 12–15.

13. G. Keil, "Venture Capital: VC-Gesellschaften müssen 'fachlich aufrüsten' und in aussichtsreiche Projekte rasch einsteigen," *Handelsblatt* (November 14, 1985), pp. B9 and B6; and "Gesucht sind 'Bauherrenmodelle' für Risikokapital," *Frankfurter Allgemeine Zeitung*, October 8, 1985, p. 14.

14. Report of the European Parliament, PE 98 518/B, June 17, 1985, p. 7.

15. C. Merbold, "Der Bürger und die Technik: Versuch einer Gruppierung," *Siemens-Zeitschrift* 57, no. 1 (1983), pp. 18–19.

7

The Legal Situation of Battered Women in the United States and West Germany

Barbara A. Reeves

For hundreds of years, laws around the world gave the man, as lord and master of his household, explicit permission to control his animals, servants, children, and wife by physical punishment. The colloquial phrase "rule of thumb" stems from old English law, where a man was expressly permitted to beat his wife provided he used a stick no thicker than his thumb.[1] In most Western countries, such laws were gradually done away with. As Western culture has remained patriarchal, however, and often continues to depict violence as commendable, even heroic, masculine behavior, the man of the house has implicit permission to maintain control of his household through the use of force.

The Scope of the Problem: Some Statistics

The family is the most venerated institution of society. The typical family is seen as the center of love and support for all of its members. The occasional sensational stories of child abuse, or husband or wife murder, have been considered rare, abnormal exceptions to the general rule of the happy, healthy family.[2] This idyllic view of the family has been exposed as a myth. Within the last twenty years, the taboo against speaking out about physical violence within the family unit has been broken. The resulting statistics are overwhelming.

The term *physical violence* can, of course, mean anything from a slap or a push to brutal torture. However, this chapter does not focus on the occasional slap during a heated argument. Rather, victims who have encountered the problems described herein have often been subjected to several months or years of regular severe beatings. Examples include being severely beaten in the face, scorched by boiling water, burned by lit cigarettes, and kicked in the stomach while pregnant.[3] Emergency-room physicians report treating battered spouses virtually every day.[4]

The literature from the United States and West Germany contains remarkably similar case histories of domestic assault victims, 95 percent of whom (in the United States) are women and children.[5] Indeed, a study of 150 countries worldwide found that familial violence against women exists in every country where the male-headed family structure prevails.[6] Moreover, the data indicate that the incidence of battering does not differ significantly from country to country. In the United States[7] and West Germany,[8] it is estimated that one out of every three wives is the victim of at least occasional physical violence on the part of her husband.

Similarly, evidence from both countries confirms that battered women come from every race, class, and socioeconomic background.[9] This reality belies the myth that only "lower-class" men beat their wives.[10] In fact, batterers, like their victims, have neither culture nor class in common. Indeed, the most consistent similarities among batterers are:

1. That they were raised in a violent home, with a father who beat either the mother or the children or both[11]

2. An attitude that they are within their rights in using physical violence against their mate[12]

3. An attitude that they should not be held responsible for their assault, either because they were drunk[13] or because the assault was provoked by the victim[14]

Providing an Alternative for Victims: The Shelter Movement

Because the man is usually the main breadwinner and authority figure within the household, a woman who is a victim of domestic assault is often economically dependent upon her assailant. This economic dependence has, in the past, made it extremely difficult or virtually impossible for the woman to leave the abusive relationship because she literally had nowhere to go. Hotels or other commercial or private lodgings were out of the question because the woman did not have the financial resources, independent of the assailant's income, to pay for them. Often, she had small children to care for, which usually precluded moving in with friends or other family members. The social stigma associated with being a "welfare case" often prevented her from going to the state for help.[15]

The Emergence of Battered Women's Shelters

As the modern-day women's movement gained international momentum in the 1960s, a new response to domestic assault emerged that involved empowering women to remove themselves from violent relationships, enabling them to make their own choices about their futures, and supporting them in their decisions. Systems of "safe houses" were organized on the grass-roots level so that female victims of violence within the family would have safe refuge from their assailants. The first such battered women's shelter was founded in Great Britain in 1971.[16] Since that time, thousands of shelters worldwide have opened their doors to women and children seeking refuge from abuse within their family units. The first U.S. shelter opened in 1972,[17] and the first West German shelter opened its doors in 1976.[18]

"Shelter Politics": A Comparison

One of the cornerstones of the feminist-inspired shelter movement is the empowerment of women to take control of their own lives and support for whatever decisions they reach. Workers in West German and U.S. shelters counsel the woman neither to terminate the relationship nor to return to it; rather, they explore all options with the woman and encourage her to reach her own decision. They also provide, with varying degrees of success depending upon the funding of the individual shelter, such services as child care, mother and child counseling, legal advice, medical assistance, and help with battling bureaucracies.

Data from West Germany[19] and the United States[20] show that in both countries more than half the women who come to a shelter for the first time return to the men who assaulted them. Despite this fact, critics of the shelter movement in both countries have labeled shelters "antifamily" because they encourage the termination of marriages. In addition, the sensationalist press has badly misinformed millions of readers. To counteract this influence, shelter workers in both countries must make community education and outreach work a major priority.

Opposition to the very concept of battered women's shelters by certain highly organized, conservative, well-financed groups[21] has caused funding to be a continual problem for shelters in both countries. In neither country have attempts to secure federal funding of shelters been successful.

The U.S. Congress has thus far declined to pass the Domestic Violence Prevention and Services bill, which would provide, inter alia, funding for programs, shelters, and community education efforts.[22] Some states, however, have passed legislation guaranteeing minimal funds to each shelter within their borders, and many cities provide additional funding and/or in-kind services, such as rent-free or low-rent space in city-owned buildings.

Even so, keeping most shelters open and able to provide a minimum of services is a constant struggle. In many shelters, the main function of the board of directors is to raise funds by means of grants, direct solicitation from various targeted groups, organization of benefits and other special events, and so forth. Private funds, raised mostly through a great expenditure of effort on the part of many volunteers, account for as much as two-thirds of the budget of the typical U.S. shelter.[23]

In West Germany, efforts to establish a federal foundation for the financing of shelters have likewise been unsuccessful. The government has declined to fund such a foundation on the ground that it is not permitted by the Basic Law.[24] However, the federal government (the Federal Ministry for Youth, Families, Women, and Health[25]) does fund programs, studies, and projects for a limited time when they are of a "model" nature—that is, when they are pioneers in a given field and when they are of nationwide relevance. For example, the ministry funded the first shelter in the country, the First Autonomous Shelter in Berlin from 1976 to 1979, and a shelter in the small town of Rendsburg from 1982 to 1985.[26]

On the state level, funding of shelters in West Germany varies as greatly as it does in the United States. Two city-states, Hamburg and Berlin, receive the best funding. The four shelters in Hamburg and three in Berlin are provided annually with a comprehensive funding package that includes personnel and operating costs. Although private donations are certainly welcomed, fundraising is not a major source of the budget. Many shelters are funded through Section 72 of the Social Service Law, which provides help for persons with "especially difficult social adjustment problems which they are unable to overcome on their own."[27] Shelter workers have consistently reported at their annual national meeting that the conservative government of Bavaria has been particularly reluctant to fund its shelters adequately.

The Response of the Criminal Justice System

Domestic assault is a crime in all fifty of the United States[28] and in West Germany.[29] The law makes no distinctions between assaults by strangers and by family members or between assaults committed in public or in the home. In reality, however, assault is generally not considered a crime if the assailant is related to the victim. Empirical evidence shows that the closer the personal relationship between the victim and the assailant, the less likely it is that the abuser will experience any negative consequences of his behavior.[30] In no other area of the criminal law is the assailant's relationship to the victim, as opposed to the severity of the offense, the most important factor in determining the response of the criminal justice system.

The ability to use violence without fear of punishment is the most important cultural facilitator of domestic assault. The historic roots of this situation are deep. Some continue to believe that the sanctity of marriage overrides the criminal law.[31] Also, women are hampered in their quest for help by the widespread phenomenon of victim blaming— the belief that a domestic assault victim is somehow "different" from other women; that she must have "asked for it"; or that she must derive some satisfaction from the battering relationship.[32] A further problem has been the continuing reluctance to view battering as a gender-related phenomenon. Instead, the response has traditionally been to examine the stresses and shortcomings of each individual relationship.

By their inaction, both the German and U.S. societies and their legal systems foster domestic abuse by reinforcing the batterer's belief that he is doing nothing wrong. Accordingly, a woman who wishes to bring her assailant to justice will likely find that his arrest is unlikely, his prosecution difficult, and his punishment, if convicted, either very lenient or completely nonexistent. Del Martin, one of the foremost authorities on domestic assault, has estimated the odds against a spouse abuse case reaching the courtroom at 100 to 1.[33]

The Police

Battered women in the United States and West Germany report remarkably similar responses on the part of the police to their calls for help. Indeed, police departments in most cities have been very slow in developing official and consistent policies for police officer response to domestic calls. If a policy exists, it has often been to *avoid* arrest if at all possible.[34] Furthermore, most police departments have been slow to offer their officers any significant training or educational programs on how to most effectively respond in an explosive domestic situation.[35] This inaction persists in spite of the horrifying statistic that at least 25 percent of all U.S. police officers killed in the line of duty are responding to domestic calls.[36]

Many women in both countries report that their calls to the police are ignored completely.[37] When the police do respond, their most common response is to attempt a reconciliation between the assailant and the victim. However, these mediation and conciliation techniques are ineffective in preventing further violence. The beatings usually begin anew, sometimes with increased severity, after the police have left.[38] Often police will walk an assailant around the block, telling him to "calm down" or to "quit drinking," and then leave. Such police conduct has been reported by women whose visible injuries were severe enough that their husbands could have been immediately arrested for aggravated or dangerous assault.[39] Women also report calling the police when their husbands are just beginning to get aggressive and being told to call back when the assault has actually occurred.[40]

A recent study by the National Institute of Justice concluded that arrest was a far more effective deterrent to repeated violence than was police mediation or separation.[41] Similar results were recorded in a 1983 study by the Police Foundation.[42] Although no comparable study appears to have been conducted in West Germany, there is every reason to believe that a policy of arrest would be just as effective a deterrent to repeated domestic abuse there as it has been in the United States.

The key element of an effective arrest policy is to empower the police to make a warrantless arrest based upon probable cause that an assault has been committed. In most U.S. jurisdictions, this requires state-enabling legislation because the general rule is that a police officer must personally witness a crime in order for a warrantless arrest to be valid. Such a requirement is ludicrous in the case of domestic assault and is obviously counterproductive to the goal of protecting the victim from further assaults. The issuance and enforcement of an arrest warrant can be a time-consuming procedure, and timely intervention is crucial to the protection of the victim. As of late 1983, thirty-three states and the District of Columbia had passed enabling legislation allowing for arrests based on probable cause.

In West Germany, police are permitted by law to arrest a suspected culprit upon their determination that an assault has been committed. Police are specifically empowered to take necessary steps to preserve the public order.[43] Nevertheless, this broad enabling law has been used very rarely as the basis for the arrest of a suspected batterer. A recently released publication recommends a critical reevaluation of the current function of the police in connection with violent conflicts within the family.[44]

The Prosecutor's Office

Even when an arrest is made, the matter is often dropped. Neither the United States nor West Germany, in their different systems of criminal procedure, accords a high priority to the prosecution of assailants. In the United States, the decision to prosecute rests ultimately with the prosecutor's office of the county where the assault occurred. A prerequisite to prosecution in most jurisdictions is that the victim sign a criminal complaint against her assailant. In most cases, a complainant may withdraw her complaint at any time before trial. If she does so, the criminal case against the defendant ends there.

Many women are reluctant to sign complaints against their abusers. There are a number of reasons for this reluctance. Economic dependence is one. In addition, many women are extremely fearful that cooperation with the authorities will lead to further abuse following the assailant's release from prison or, if he has already been released on bond, following notification of continued criminal proceedings against him. Often, an assailant threatens to "get even" if his victim presses charges. This psychological abuse is often very effective in deterring women from following through on a criminal complaint because they understandably have little or no expectation that the law enforcement system will protect them from further assaults.[45]

In many cases, women who are willing, even eager, to press charges against their assailant are discouraged from doing so by the prosecutor's office.[46] Many prosecutors still believe that intrafamily relations, even when violent, are private and do not warrant interference by the prosecutor's office. Or they may regard physical violence within marriage as "normal" and not a crime.[47] Because a prosecutor's decision not to prosecute a case is generally not subject to review in either country, a woman who is stopped by an uncooperative prosecutor has no recourse other than to sue her assailant privately: an expensive and time-consuming procedure in both countries.

On the other hand, prosecutors eager to pursue spouse abuse cases are often frustrated by a victim either declining to sign a criminal complaint or deciding to withdraw her complaint after the process has been started. In a few U.S. cities, prosecutors have attempted to remedy this problem by instituting "no drop" prosecution policies. This means that the victim of a domestic assault no longer has the unfettered option to withdraw her complaint once it has been filed. In those jurisdictions where policies sensitive to victims' situations have been developed,[48] successful prosecutions of suspected abusers have increased.

Where the responsibility for prosecution is shifted from the victim to the prosecutor's office, women will by and large be more willing to see a prosecution through. The woman then no longer has the burden of signing the complaint and being labeled "the complainant." Rather, the complaint may be signed by the police officer who responded to the call, and the woman's role becomes solely that of a witness. Many women are less likely to fear reprisal by their assailant under such a policy because the defendant is informed that the victim does not have the right to refuse prosecution or to drop the charges.[49]

In West Germany, the laws covering domestic abuse differentiate according to the severity of the abuse. Prosecutorial procedure varies accordingly. There exist under present law three categories of offense:

Privatklagedelikte are analogous to civil tort suits in the United States and require the victim to assume full responsibility for the case. The prosecutor (*Staatsanwalt*) does not become involved. "Simple assault" is such an offense.[50]

Antragsdelikte require the victim to file an application to have the case taken by the prosecutor. This requirement is roughly analogous to the criminal complaint requirement in the United States. The victim is free to withdraw the application at any time prior to the end of the criminal proceedings. Once the application has been withdrawn, it cannot be refiled, and all pending criminal proceedings against the defendant cease immediately.[51] "Dangerous assault" and all forms of property damage are examples of cases normally requiring an application.[52]

An exception to this rule exists if the prosecuting attorney makes a determination that a "special public interest" (*besonderes öffentliches Interesse*) is present, which justifies a prosecution without an application from and follow-through by the victim. However, it is solely within the prosecutor's discretion to determine when such a public interest exists. Despite the efforts of activists and shelter workers encouraging prosecutors to recognize a "special public interest" in curbing domestic violence, only rarely will a case be prosecuted in this fashion.[53]

Offizialdelikte require action by the prosecution independently of the action (or inaction) of the victim. Only "serious assault," attempted murder, and related offenses fall into this category.[54]

In both the United States and West Germany, prosecution of wife abusers continues to be a low priority in most jurisdictions. In the year 1984, prosecutions for theft in West Germany outnumbered prosecutions for physical assault six to one.[55] Similarly, in the United States, a thief or burglar is much more likely to be prosecuted than a wife abuser.[56] This is a rare exception to the general rule that violent crimes are sanctioned more than property crimes.[57]

The Judiciary

It is well recognized that certainty of punishment, rather than severity of punishment, is the most effective deterrent to criminal behavior.[58] Jail or prison terms are permissible sentences for assault convictions in all of West Germany and in most jurisdictions in the United States.[59] Judges, however, in the exercise of their discretionary powers, often present yet another hurdle for women seeking to bring their assailants to justice. Many judges, like their colleagues in the police department and the prosecutor's office, continue to believe that the courtroom is not the proper arena for the resolution of domestic disputes, no matter how violent.[60] Accordingly, the court often uses the "judicial process to conciliate rather than adjudicate."[61] Moreover, many judges view the defendant's relationship to the victim as a mitigating factor. "When the abuser in a domestic violence incident is convicted, the judge's consideration of the relationship between the parties often results in a sentence less severe than the offense would warrant."[62] Referral to mediation, or nominal fines, neither of which requires an admission of guilt by the defendant, are commonplace.[63]

The System Begins to Respond: Positive Developments

In just fifteen years, the battered women's movement has effected considerable societal change in both West Germany and the United States. Public reaction to victims of domestic violence who have broken the long-standing taboo against speaking out has measurably improved. Battered women's shelters have gained legitimacy. Their value and necessity are no longer seriously doubted. Those who questioned the need for shelters have been silenced by the statistics. In West Germany, for example, it was estimated in 1986 that 24,000 women annually seek refuge in the country's more than 150 shelters.[64]

Until the past few years, the focus has been on the victim of domestic assault instead of on the assailant. To the oft-repeated question "Why does she stay?" the shelter movement responded, "Because she has nowhere to go." It is now at least possible, although still difficult, for a battered woman to leave the violent situation. Only very recently has the far more appropriate question—"Why does he batter?"—been addressed. "Because our system allows it and even encourages it" is the answer that both West Germany and the United States are now being forced to recognize.

In West Germany, a literary study entitled "Violence Against Women— Causes and Possibilities for Intervention" has recently been published. This study was commissioned and funded by the federal government.[65] Also under consideration is a series of domestic violence education seminars for police officers and prosecuting attorneys. Legislation has been introduced to make rape within marriage a crime. Concerned men have begun organizing to prevent domestic violence as well. In Hamburg, Männer gegen Männergewalt (Men Against Male Violence), the first and still the only group of its kind, began offering group therapy sessions in 1985 for batterers who wished to change their behavior.[66]

In the United States, men's groups in several cities now offer therapy programs for batterers.[67] For the most part, participation in them is voluntary. Another recent approach, however, has been to offer a convicted spouse abuser probation instead of a jail term on the condition that he participate in a counseling program. The U.S. Commission on Civil Rights found this can be effective in preventing future violence: "In cases where the pattern of abuse has not yet resulted in serious injury, and where abusers genuinely desire to alter their behavior and have the additional motivation of incarceration for failure to do so counseling may help them learn how to handle stress without resorting to violence."[68]

One multidimensional project that combines and coordinates the efforts of the police, prosecutor's office, judiciary, mental health system, and the community at large is the Domestic Abuse Intervention Project, started in Duluth, Minnesota, by Ellen Pence in 1980. Under this project, there is a police policy of mandatory arrest upon determination of probable cause that an assault has been committed. When a defendant is released pending prosecution, he is under court order not to harass his victim in any way. The arresting officer is the complainant, and the policy is to prosecute. The victim is given an advocate who helps her throughout the criminal process. Judges have agreed to offer probation in lieu of a jail term to convicted first offenders if they take advantage of available counseling. Attendance at ten of twelve sessions is required; if more than two sessions are missed, a probation revocation hearing is called.[69]

The incidence of arrest, prosecution, and conviction of wife beaters has increased greatly since the advent of the project. Although no data are yet available on the percentage of assailants who are successfully rehabilitated, the consistent and concerted response of Duluth certainly serves notice to wife beaters that their violence will not be tolerated by the community.

Strategies for the Future

The following is a list of suggestions for a more effective societal response to batterers and their victims:

- Use of the police power to arrest suspected batterers should be expanded. Police departments in both countries should develop policies of mandatory arrest upon determination of probable cause that an assault has been committed. Such policies have the dual benefit of punishing the assailant's conduct and putting the victim, at least temporarily, out of danger.

- When an assailant is released from custody, pending prosecution or other proceedings, he should be enjoined from all harassment. Bond should be revoked, or other sanctions imposed, if he violates the injunction.

- Suspected assailants should be prosecuted more consistently in both countries. In West Germany, prosecutors should recognize the special public interest in domestic assault cases. In the United States, "no drop" prosecution policies should be encouraged in more jurisdictions.

- Members of the criminal justice system should be provided with additional seminars and courses on domestic violence.

- Education programs for the community at large should be expanded in both countries. For this purpose, there should be funding for additional personnel, so that shelter workers do not have to take time away from direct work with shelter residents and their children.

- Therapy programs for batterers should be expanded. These programs can be valuable in effecting behavior modification because, even while condemning his behavior, they offer the batterer a nonviolent alternative. West Germany should consider making participation in such programs a condition of probation in selected cases. This practice should also be expanded in the United States.

- More multidimensional projects modeled after the Duluth Domestic Abuse Intervention Project should be organized.

- Finally, financial and political support for battered women's shelters must continue to increase in both countries. Funding must become more secure, especially in the United States, so that workers may put more of their energies into substantive work rather than into raising enough money to keep the shelter doors open.

Conclusion

The consequences of allowing domestic violence to go unchecked are becoming ever more apparent: Close to one-third of all homicides in the United States are killings within the family.[70] Moreover, there is a danger that the statistics will increase exponentially from generation to generation because children who grow up in violent homes are more likely to become batterers or victims as adults.[71] Another potential consequence of denying battered women ready access to help is that, in desperation, they sometimes take the law into their own hands. The media have recently reported on longtime victims of abuse who have ultimately defended themselves with deadly force.[72]

The United States and West Germany can learn a great deal from each other in their efforts to go beyond "providing the ambulance at the bottom of the cliff." Now that both countries have recognized the need for preventive measures, the difficult task of effecting changes of attitude and practice on the part of their criminal justice systems can be undertaken on a bilateral, even international, level. Perhaps this chapter can provide some guidance.

Acknowledgments

The author thanks Renate Augstein, Pamela Selwyn, and Christine Alderdissen.

Notes

1. W. Blackstone, *Commentaries on the Laws of England* (1765), as quoted in *Under the Rule of Thumb: Battered Women and the Administration of Justice* (Washington, D.C.: U.S. Commission on Civil Rights, 1982), p. 2.

2. S. Steinmetz and M. Straus, eds., *Violence in the Family* (New York: Dodd, Mead, 1975), p. 6.

3. *Frauen gegen Männergewalt*, Berliner Frauenhaus für misshandelte Frauen—Erster Erfahrungsbericht (Berlin: Frauen Selbstverlag, 1978), p. 16.

4. S. Eisenberg and P. Micklow, "The Assaulted Wife: 'Catch 22' Revisited," *Women's Rights Law Reporter* 3 (Spring-Summer 1977), p. 141.

5. U.S. Department of Justice, *Report to the Nation on Crime and Justice: The Data* (Washington, D.C.: Government Printing Office, 1983).

6. F. Hosken, *Wife Abuse and Violence Against Women: A World View* (London: Women's International Network, 1984).

7. M. Straus, R. Gelles, and S. Steinmetz, *Behind Closed Doors: Violence in the American Family* (New York: Anchor Books, 1980), p. 32.

8. E. Neubauer, U. Steinbrecher, and S. Drescher-Aldendorff, *Gewalt gegen Frauen: Ursachen und Interventionsmöglichkeiten*, vol. 212, Schriftenreihe des Bundesministers für Jugend, Familie, Frauen, und Gesundheit (Stuttgart: Verlag Kohlhammer, 1987), p. 7.

9. D. Martin, *Battered Wives* (New York: Simon and Schuster, 1976), p. 20.

10. Of recent notoriety was the case of John Fedders, a high-ranking attorney at the Securities and Exchange Commission in Washington, D.C., who was forced to resign after public disclosure that he had been regularly beating his wife for years.

11. R. Gelles, "Abused Wives: Why Do They Stay?" *Journal of Marriage and the Family* 38 (1976), pp. 659–668.

12. D. Ohl and U. Rösener, *Und bist Du nicht willig . . . so brauch Ich gewalt: Ausmass und Ursachen von Frauenmisshandlung in der Familie* (Frankfurt: Ullstein Materialien, 1979), p. 85.

13. Studies unanimously show that although alcohol is often present, it does not cause violence. Rather, the assailant drinks in order to provide himself an excuse for his violent behavior. Ibid., at 55.

14. One commentator made the following comparison: "To claim that women provoke the violence of which they are so often victim is to argue that Jewish passivity invited genocide." L. Pogrebin, "Do Women Make Men Violent?" *Ms.* (November 1974), p. 37.

15. This attitude is reported less often in West Germany, where the social welfare system is much more responsive to the needs of the poor than that of the United States.

16. L. Walker, *The Battered Woman* (New York: Harper & Row, 1979), p. 192.

17. S. Schechter, *Women and Male Violence: The Visions and Struggles of the Battered Women's Movement* (Boston: South End Press, 1982), p. 62.

18. *Frauen gegen Männergewalt,* p. 16.

19. *Hilfen für misshandelte Frauen,* vol. 124, Schriftenreihe des Bundesministers für Jugend, Familie, und Gesundheit (Stuttgart: Verlag Kohlhammer, 1981), p. 144.

20. Walker, *The Battered Woman,* p. 199.

21. Right-wing activist Phyllis Schlafly was instrumental in the defeat of the Domestic Violence Prevention and Services bill; see Schechter, *Women and Male Violence,* p. 147.

22. Ibid.

23. Ibid., pp. 86–87.

24. "Droht das Aus für's Frauenhaus?" (Göttingen: Zentrale Informationsstelle für Autonome Frauenhäuser, 1985).

25. The ministry added "women" to its name when it expanded its women's policy section in 1986.

26. Study results confirmed that rural women experience essentially the same difficulties as those from the cities.

27. Bundessozialhilfegesetz section 72 provides that "Personen, bei denen besondere soziale Schwierigkeiten der Teilnahme am Leben in der Gemeinschaft entgegenstehen, ist Hilfe zur überwindung dieser Schwierigkeiten zu gewähren, wenn sie aus eigener Kraft hierzu nicht fähig sind." (Persons with especially difficult social adjustment problems that they are unable to overcome on their own are entitled to aid.) This form of funding has been widely criticized because the funding level of each shelter becomes dependent on the number of women seeking refuge there. That is, a certain minimum number of women must be abused in order for funding to remain at a consistent, adequate level (Ohl and Rösener, *Und bist Du nicht willig,* p. 203).

28. *Under the Rule of Thumb,* p. 2.

29. Strafgesetzbuch (StGB), Section 223 *et seq.*

30. *Under the Rule of Thumb,* p. 24.

31. Eisenberg and Micklow, "The Assaulted Wife," p. 158.

32. E. Pence, *The Justice System's Response to Domestic Violence Cases: A Guide for Policy Development* (Duluth: Minnesota Program Development, 1985), pp. 4–5.

33. *Under the Rule of Thumb*, p. 36.

34. In 1974, the police policy in Wayne County, Michigan, was as follows:

    a. Avoid arrest if possible. Appeal to their vanity.
    b. Explain the procedure of obtaining a warrant.
       1) Complainant must sign complaint.
       2) Must appear in court.
       3) Consider loss of time.
       4) Cost of court.
    c. State that your only interest is to prevent a breach of the peace.
    d. Explain that attitudes usually change by court time.
    e. Recommend a postponement.
       1) Court not in session.
       2) No judge available.
    f. *Don't* be too harsh or critical.

(Cited in Eisenberg and Micklow, "The Assaulted Wife," pp. 156–157.)

35. Ibid., p. 156.

36. Walker, *The Battered Woman*, p. 208.

37. *Under the Rule of Thumb*, p. 21; *Frauen gegen Männergewalt*, pp. 100–102. In the 1983 Oregon case of *Nearing v. Weaver, Sauls and the City of St. Helens*, 205 Or. 702, 670 P.2d 137 (1983), the Supreme Court of Oregon held that a mother and children victimized by domestic assault had a cause of action against the police department and individual officers who, in disregard of a court restraining order issued against the father under the state's Abuse Prevention Law, failed to arrest that person despite probable cause that he was continuing his assaults. In *Thurman v. City of Torrington*, 595 F. Supp. 1521 (1984), a woman recovered $2.6 million in her damage suit against the city and its police department, which had consistently failed to respond to her calls for help. In that case, a federal district court in Connecticut held that plaintiff's constitutional right of equal protection was violated because the police policy did not accord the same diligence of response to cases of domestic abuse as it did to cases of abuse not involving a domestic relationship.

38. *Under the Rule of Thumb*, p. 21; *Frauen gegen Männergewalt*, pp. 100–102.

39. *Under the Rule of Thumb*, p. 19.

40. *Frauen gegen Männergewalt*, p. 100.

41. Pence, *The Justice System's Response*, p. 7.

42. L. Sherman and R. Berk, *Police Responses to Domestic Assault: Preliminary Findings* (Washington, D.C.: Police Foundation, 1983).

43. Section 14, Allgemeines Sicherheits und Ordnungsgesetz—the group of statutes defining the rights of the police department.

44. Neubauer et al., *Gewalt gegen Frauen*, p. 100.

45. In a recent Michigan case, an abuser who repeatedly assaulted and threatened his wife was released on bail despite the court's knowledge of the threats. The same day he was released, he returned to the marital residence and shot his wife to death before committing suicide. *Detroit Free Press*, November 20, 1985, p. 3.

46. *Under the Rule of Thumb*, p. 24.

47. The author once accompanied a resident of the Berlin shelter to file a complaint against her husband, who had stabbed her twice in the shoulder. The *female* officer asked the woman if she really wanted to prosecute; after all, "things like this happen occasionally in every marriage" ("Sowas kommt doch in jeder Ehe 'mal vor").

48. It is important for the success of such policies to avoid imposing sanctions against those victims who steadfastly refuse to cooperate in the prosecution of their assailants. The reasons for such refusals are often complex, and a policy that includes contempt-of-court proceedings for a victim who declines to cooperate amounts to another form of victim blaming. "'No-Drop' Prosecution Policies Sometimes Backfire Against Victims," *Response to Violence in the Family and Sexual Assault* 7, no. 3 (May-June 1984), p. 13.

49. *Under the Rule of Thumb*, p. 38.

50. StGB, Section 223.

51. StGB, Section 77d.

52. StGB, Sections 223a; 232.

53. *Hilfen für Misshandelte Frauen*, p. 115.

54. StGB, Section 224 *et. seq.*

55. Bundeskriminalamt, *Kriminalstatistik* (Wiesbaden: Kriminalistisches Institut, 1984), pp. 89–95.

56. *Under the Rule of Thumb*, p. 32.

57. In both the U.S. and West Germany, for example, armed robbery is a more serious crime than burglary.

58. W. LaFave and A. Scott, *Criminal Law* (Chicago: West Publishing, 1980), p. 88.

59. StGB, Section 223 *et seq.*; *Under the Rule of Thumb*, p. 59.

60. *Under the Rule of Thumb*, p. 57.

61. Ibid., p. 37.

62. Ibid., p. 43.

63. Eisenberg and Micklow, "The Assaulted Wife," p. 150.

64. Heubauer et al., *Gewalt gegen Frauen*, p. 7.

65. Ibid.

66. Ibid., p. 96.

67. Ibid.

68. *Under the Rule of Thumb*, p. 96.

69. Pence, *The Justice System's Response*, pp. 12–43.

70. Eisenberg and Micklow, "The Assaulted Wife," p. 141.

71. *Under the Rule of Thumb*, p. 97.

72. The made-for-TV-movie "The Burning Bed," in which a wife who had been battered for years was acquitted of murder charges after killing her husband by setting the house on fire while he slept, was based on the 1977 case of *People* v. *Francine Hughes*. The story of Francine Hughes was also documented in F. McNulty, *The Burning Bed* (New York: Harcourt Brace Jovanovich, 1980).

8

Document Production in the Federal Republic of Germany: Progress and Problems

A. Bradley Shingleton

International judicial assistance has always been faced with the problem of reconciling international treaty obligations with domestic law. Some of the most difficult issues in this respect have been procedural ones, particularly those connected with pretrial discovery. In the United States, the recent U.S. Supreme Court decision in *Societe Nationale Industrielle Aerospatiale* v. *U.S. District Court for the Southern District of Iowa*[1] revealed a deep division in the highest U.S. court concerning the nature and extent of international obligations when they directly conflict with the jurisdictional power of U.S. courts.

An analogous debate is occurring in West Germany concerning the pretrial discovery of documents by foreign litigants in that country. Although a signatory of the Hague Convention On Obtaining Evidence Abroad,[2] the West German government exercised a reservation under Article 23 of the convention against the execution of requests for pretrial document discovery. Now, however, the government is preparing a regulation that would permit document discovery to occur in its territory. In light of the increasing pressure of extraterritorial discovery orders by U.S. courts and a growing number of product liability claims in the United States against German manufacturers and exporters, the draft regulation prepared by the German Ministry of Justice (Bundesministerium der Justiz, hereafter BMJ) has been intensively discussed and revised. The activity expanded to another front in January 1987 when a group of German industry counsel, dissatisfied with the BMJ draft, formed a working group to produce an alternative draft regulation that is more sympathetic to German industrial interests. Both drafts, along with brief explanatory commentaries by their respective authors, are

117

now circulating among representatives of industry, government, and the bar in Germany.

The Context of the Regulations

The regulations seek to permit for the first time the "pretrial discovery of documents" in West Germany pursuant to the Hague Evidence Convention. As of December 31, 1987, The Hague Evidence Convention had been ratified by twenty states, including the United States (March 1972) and West Germany (June 1979). According to Article 23 of the Convention, "A Contracting State may at the time of signature, ratification or accession, declare that it will not execute Letters of Request issued for the purpose of obtaining pre-trial discovery of documents as known in Common Law countries."[3]

Only four signatory states, among them the United States, have not exercised this right of reservation; most European countries have done so. West Germany declared its reservation under Article 23 in its domestic legislation implementing the convention, commonly known as the Implementation Act of December 22, 1977. The act stated that West Germany was declaring a reservation under Article 23 because the "exploratory character" of document discovery was alien to its system of civil procedure. The Implementation Act went on to provide in Article 14:

> However, to the extent that the fundamental principles of the German Law of Procedure are not violated, such requests may be granted considering the justified interests of the persons involved, after the requirements for the granting of such requests and the applicable procedure have been implemented by Regulations which the Minister of Justice with the consent of the Bundesrat [upper House of Parliament] may issue.[4]

Diverse motives impelled the majority of the signatory states to declare an Article 23 reservation, but in essence those declarations arose out of a reluctance to permit a wide-ranging discovery procedure, alien to their systems of civil litigation, to be utilized within their sovereign territories.[5] In the past several years, however, a countertrend has manifested itself, and some states, such as the United Kingdom and France, have softened their Article 23 reservations in order to permit some document production requests to be executed. This countermovement is fueled by a growing perception that the convention is seriously threatened with irrelevance or paralysis if the majority of its signatories refuse to provide any means for the discovery of documents, which the U.S. Supreme Court described in *Aerospatiale* as "a staple of international litigation."[6] This sense of crisis, perceptible from the record of the 1985 meeting of the signatory states on the operation of the convention, has provided a strong impetus for the West German government to accelerate the preparation of a document-production regulation.

The Procedural Context of the Problem

It is impossible to understand the procedural context of the proposed regulations without an appreciation of some of the distinctive features of German civil procedure. A number of recent articles in English contain concise presentations of its basic principles, so we will restrict our attention to four characteristics that have particular relevance for the proposed regulations.[7]

Judicial Management of Fact Gathering

A German judge, unlike his or her U.S. counterpart, has the primary responsibility for defining the factual issues of a case and deciding which pieces of evidence described in the pleadings should be examined by the court at a hearing or in camera.[8] Jury trials are essentially unknown in German civil procedure, so the judge operates as a fact-finder as well as an arbiter.[9] Counsel for the parties can, of course, urge the judge to consider specific pieces of evidence, but the judge alone ultimately decides what evidence is relevant and will be received. He or she conducts the essential questioning of the witnesses and the inspection of documents and other tangible evidence and controls the other means of taking evidence.[10] U.S.-style document discovery, privately conducted without direct judicial supervision, stands in radical contrast to the fundamental principles of the judicial conduct of fact gathering and of the judicial evaluation of evidence in West German procedure. Additionally, German civil procedure does not divide the course of litigation into discovery and trial phases. Instead, fact gathering and fact evaluation occur simultaneously. For these and other reasons, the institution of discovery is essentially unknown in German courts.[11]

Limited Power to Compel Production of Documents

The power to compel production of documents in West German procedure is, generally speaking, much more limited than in U.S. procedure. Because there is no pretrial discovery as such between German litigants, a party has no right to obtain the production of all documents relevant to the action, much less those that may lead to the discovery of admissible evidence. In fact, a German party is entitled to obtain a document from his or her opponent only if the document is material and the opponent has either referred to the document in a pleading[12] or is obligated to produce the document under a provision of substantive law.[13] The court's ability to order production of documents *sua sponte* is limited to certain kinds of documents, such as public records.[14] In the event a party refuses to comply with an order for production, a judge has the right to draw inferences about the content of the document and accept the opponent's contentions about the document. Otherwise, the court has no general power to sanction noncompliance with a production order.

With respect to a document in possession of a nonparty, a litigant may only compel production when he or she has a right to the document under substantive law.[15] In the event the nonparty fails to produce the document, the requesting party must file suit against him or her.[16] Documents cannot, therefore, be easily acquired in German litigation, with the exception of documents directly at issue in the litigation. This is the result of a different model of litigation in German procedure, as well as much more stringent criteria of relevance and materiality.

Relevance and Materiality

The German concept of relevance is significantly more limited than that in U.S. law. This results primarily from two factors: (1) the tendency of German procedure to focus and concentrate on disputed issues and to disregard issues that have no bearing on the outcome of the case,[17] and (2) judicial conduct of fact-finding. Because the German judge is responsible for determining the facts and applying the law to the facts, he or she quickly concentrates efforts on the issues that appear to be dispositive. Or, as one writer has expressed it, "He is constantly looking for the jugular."[18] Relevant evidence in the German system of litigation is evidence that promotes the resolution of a case. When this concept is combined with the judicial conduct of fact gathering, the result is much more limited than the concept of relevance embodied in Rule 26 of the Federal Rules of Civil Procedure. The harmonization of the U.S. and German concepts of relevance presents one of the most difficult problems in the regulations.

Evidentiary Privileges

Generally speaking, German law manifests a greater concern than U.S. law does for the protection of confidential information in litigation.[19] The privileges available to a German witness, which primarily arise out of his or her personal or professional relationships, basically resemble testimonial privileges in the United States. The protection of business and industrial information, however, is more extensive in Germany. Sections 384 and 383 of the Code of Civil Procedure (Zivilprozessordnung, hereafter ZPO) permit a witness to refuse to disclose information concerning business secrets belonging to him (or her) or others. Additionally, some provisions of substantive law, such as Section 404 of the Stock Corporation Act (Aktiengesellschaftsgesetz), provide for criminal punishment for unauthorized disclosure of an industrial secret.[20] These provisions are constitutionally anchored in the so-called rule of law clause of the German Basic Law (Grundgesetz), according to which "the rights of personal privacy, commercial property and business secrets may not be interfered with unless such interference is necessary to protect other persons' rights in the course of civil litigation."[21] The presumption of secrecy in German law, in short, is contrary to the basic notion contained in the Federal Rules of Civil Procedure in which an evidentiary privilege is not presumed, but must be affirmatively asserted by the party resisting discovery.

The Proposed Regulations

The BMJ and the industry drafts have evolved quite differently. The earliest version of the BMJ draft dates from 1983, but it met with a lukewarm reception, thus causing further work on it to proceed slowly. The initial concern of industry at that time has since become a recurring objection: the regulation was a one-sided concession that offered U.S. litigants an additional means for procuring evidence without obliging them to use it.

Because of substantial dissatisfaction with the BMJ draft, a group of industry legal counsel representing some of the largest German industrial concerns formed a working group to propose revisions to the BMJ draft. The group retained Karl M. Meessen,[22] professor of international law in Augsburg, to assist them. The industry group and Meessen were concerned that the BMJ draft violated several basic principles of German procedural and substantive law and therefore exceeded the authorization of Article 14 of the Implementation Act for enactment of a regulation. The group also felt that it went too far in accommodating U.S. interests and procedure in that it permitted the execution, viewed from the German perspective, of excessively broad requests. Furthermore, permitting U.S.-style discovery would favor foreign litigants over domestic ones and would entail the violation of German constitutional and procedural principles.

A fundamental contrast in purpose between the two drafts must be noted at the outset. The purpose of the BMJ draft, as stated in its commentary, is to permit, "in principle," the execution of Letters of Request for the pretrial discovery of documents[23]—in other words, to accommodate foreign procedure as much as possible. The industry draft, in contrast, emphasizes that it provides for the production of documents under the procedures of German law. In support of this position, it appeals to the Hague Evidence Convention, which in Article 12 neither requires nor authorizes changes in the internal law of a signatory state.[24]

The two proposed regulations can best be analyzed by comparing them on three major points: (1) specificity requirements, (2) procedure, and (3) evidentiary privileges.

Specificity Requirements

The requirements for specificity in a document request are perhaps the most important and controversial provisions in each draft. The BMJ draft embodies more general criteria that are primarily directed to the Letter of Request, whereas the industry draft applies its specificity criteria to the pleadings in the action as well. The purpose of specificity criteria in both versions is clearly to restrict production to documents that relate to specific allegations and ultimate issues and to prohibit production where it may facilitate the discovery of additional claims for relief. The relevant specificity criteria are:

BMJ
- Sufficient designation of documents
- Discernible connection between the documents and the subject matter of the case

Industry
- Definite claim in the action
- Sufficiently specific factual contentions
- Clearly discernible connection between contentions and documents requested[25]

The looser criteria of the BMJ draft would clearly permit execution of a greater number of requests. From the industry perspective, however, the BMJ criteria are excessively "wide-meshed."[26] According to the industry critique, they create, in effect, a duty to produce that is unfounded in German law and that violates the German constitutional principles of proportionality (Article 1 of the Basic Law) and of equal treatment of foreign and domestic litigants (Article 3 of the Basic Law).[27] The difficulty of harmonizing German and U.S. concepts of relevance lies at the heart of the discovery controversy and reveals the contrasting biases of the two systems of litigation.

Procedure

The drafts provide for significantly different treatment of production requests directed to third parties. Although neither version expands the obligation of a third person to produce documents beyond that in the ZPO, they diverge on the issue of sanctions against a third person when production is refused. The BMJ draft departs from normal ZPO procedure to permit direct sanctions in the form of a fine or imprisonment against a person obligated to produce documents under ZPO sections 422 and 429.[28] Normal ZPO procedure requires that a party file a separate civil action against the third person. The commentary to the BMJ draft reasons that this leaves U.S. litigants no better off than if the regulation or the Hague Convention did not exist. Because the purpose of the convention is to promote international judicial assistance, the BMJ drafters assert that a German judge should be given the same powers to compel production as he or she has to compel testimony.

In contrast, the industry draft does not specifically address production by a third party. It provides merely that "to the extent a request for assistance is to be executed as the result of an enforceable decision rendered in accordance with paragraph 1 above, the executing judge executes the request without delay according to the modes of German law."[29] In the commentary to the industry draft, Meessen stated that because the guiding principle of that draft is to provide judicial assistance without changing internal German law, production from a third person should proceed under the regulation as it does under normal procedure.[30] Consequently, no powers to sanction nonproduction by a third person are provided in the industry draft. Such a provision is not, in his opinion, consistent with the Implementation Act of 1977 or with constitutional principles of equality and equal protection. Whatever the merits of this view, if it prevails, third-party production will be perceived in the United States as a toothless procedure. Nevertheless, because U.S. courts and litigants have no choice but to proceed under the regulation when seeking documents from third persons, whatever procedure is ultimately adopted will have to be tolerated.

Evidentiary Privileges

A final major area in which the drafts differ concerns evidentiary privilege. The BMJ text only contains one reference to this in Article 1, in which its states that production will only be permitted, inter alia, where there are no countervailing interests of the producing party worthy of protection. Cited as examples of such interests are industrial and business secrets. The industry draft, on the other hand, contains two broad provisions that refer to evidentiary privileges. Article 1 rejects requests that would violate other applicable laws, or "personal interests worthy of protection." Article 3(3) incorporates this prohibition and expands it by explicitly recognizing privileges available under the law of the requesting state, as permitted by Article 11 of the Hague Evidence Convention. In speaking of the interests of "affected persons" rather than "producing party," the range of potential objectors is much greater in the industry draft because it would presumably include persons in whose interest a document was created.[31]

Although this position may be compatible with German law, it appears overly protective from the U.S. perspective. The privacy interests of third persons in the United States are typically protected by protective orders. The more critical issue is how a German judge would balance the right to privacy with the right to discovery. As noted, evidentiary privileges are more extensive in Germany than in the United States, and they are accorded greater weight. A U.S. court could pressure a Geman defendant into waiving all German privileges in exchange for requiring use of the Hague Evidence Convention, but this does not solve the underlying problem. The only way to give U.S. litigants a sense of fair treatment is to limit the application of German privileges to those cases in which they outweigh the right to production, essentially as the BMJ text does. This would imply an alteration of German procedure. Full recognition of German privileges, however, would undoubtedly deter U.S. courts from ordering use of the regulation for fear of severe limitation of a party's right to discovery.

This issue reveals again the differing objectives of the two drafts. The BMJ draft attempts to promote the execution of production requests. Its limits are in the areas where fundamental principles are affected or where concerned persons are unreasonably burdened.[32] The basic notion of the industry proposal is that requests should be executed only "when they satisfy the presuppositions that must be observed when documentary evidence is produced in German law. . . . The jurisdiction and procedures of central authorities are [in this draft] merely supplemented, not changed."[33] Accordingly, production must occur under the procedures of German law.[34]

Prospects

What are the prospects for a German document-production regulation at present? One proposed alternative to the issuance of a regulation is a bilateral treaty between Germany and the United States. But it is hard to see what incentives the United States has to agree to a restrictive procedure for document production outside of a multilateral convention. A German blocking statute prohibiting document production would appear unavailing in view of the fate that other such acts have experienced in U.S. courts. The status quo in the wake of *Aerospatiale* is unstable. The balancing test dictated by that case appears unlikely to be applied with consistency and predictability or to be applied inoffensively to German parties.

The remaining alternative, therefore, is a regulation, and the authors of both of the present drafts appear to favor this alternative. Which of the two versions will be enacted remains to be seen, but it appears that industry, with its considerable political clout, will support the industry version. Whether the BMJ draft will ultimately include some elements of the industry proposal is essentially a political question. Because most of the state justice ministries purportedly support the BMJ draft, the final regulation, if enacted, will likely bear a close resemblance to it.

Viewed from the U.S. perspective, a workable regulation should be welcomed because it would establish a definite procedure where none exists. In order to be palatable to U.S. courts, however, the regulation must be sufficiently liberal so that a requesting party is given a fair opportunity to accumulate documents necessary for the preparation of litigation. If the version enacted does not provide this in the form of a reliable and economical procedure, the jurisdictional conflicts in international discovery between the United States and West Germany may continue.

Notes

1. 107 S.Ct. 2542, 96 L.Ed.2d 461 (1987).

2. The Hague Convention on the Taking of Evidence Abroad in Civil or Commercial Matters, March 18, 1970, 23 U.S.T. 2555, T.I.A.S. No. 744, 847 U.N.T.S. 231, codified at 28 U.S.C.A. Section 1781.

3. Ibid., Article 23.

4. "Gesetz zur Ausführung des Hager Übereinkommens vom 15. November 1965 über die Zustellung gerichtlicher und aussergerichtlicher Schriftstücke im Ausland in Zivil- oder Handelssachen und die Beweisaufnahme im Ausland in Zivil- oder Handelssachen vom 22. Dezember 1977" (Implementation Act), Artikel 14, Bundesgesetzblatt I, 3106. An English translation of the entire act appears in B. A. Ristau, 2 *International Judicial Assistance (Civil and Commercial)* 82 (1986).

5. Restatement (Revised) of the Foreign Relations Law of the United States, section 437, Reporter's note 1 (Tentative Draft no. 7, April 10, 1986), approved May 14, 1986, in which it is stated: "No aspect of the extension of the American legal system beyond the territorial frontier of the United States has given rise to so much friction as the request for documents associated with investigation and litigation in the United States."

On the origin of Article 23 in the drafting of the Hague Convention, see generally P. Amram, "U.S. Ratification of the Hague Convention on Taking Evidence Abroad," 67 *Am. J. Int. L.* 104 (1973).

6. See note 1.

7. See generally D. Gerber, "Extraterritorial Discovery: Cooperation, Coercion and the Hague Evidence Convention," 19 *Vand. J. Int. L.* 739 (1986); J. Langbein, "The German Advantage in Civil Procedure," 52 *U. Chi. L. R.* 823 (1985); P. Gottwald, "Simplified Civil Procedure in West Germany," 31 *Am. J. Comp. L.* 687 (1983); also see the older classic article by B. Kaplan, A. von Mehren, and R. Schaefer, "Phases of German Civil Procedure," 71 *Harv. L. Rev.* 1193, 1443 (1958).

8. This is the so-called duty of clarification, which is imposed on the court by section 139 of the Zivilprozessordnung (Code of Civil Procedure, hereafter ZPO). See generally L. Rosenberg and K. Schwab, *Zivilprozessrecht*, 13th ed. (Munich: C. H. Beck Verlag, 1981), pp. 437–440.

9. Gerber, "Extraterritorial Discovery," p. 753. Professor Langbein saw the judicial conduct of fact gathering as the "grand discriminant" between German and American legal culture. Langbein, "The German Advantage," p. 863.

10. ZPO, section 397.

11. For more on the discontinuous sequence of German litigation in which fact-finding and fact evaluation occur simultaneously, see Langbein, "The German Advantage," p. 830 ff.

12. ZPO, section 423.

13. ZPO, section 422.

14. ZPO, sections 142, 272b.

15. ZPO, section 429.

16. ZPO, sections 429–431.

17. Langbein, "The German Advantage," pp. 830–832.

18. Ibid., p. 832. Gerber, "Extraterritorial Discovery," p. 753.

19. On this point, see R. Stürner, "Die gewerbliche Geheimsphäre im Zivilprozess, 10 *Juristen Zeitung* 453 (1985); P. Schlosser, "Internationale Rechtshilfe und rechtsstaatlicher Schutz von Beweispersonen," 94 *Zeitschrift für Zivilprozess* 369 (1981); Gerber, ibid., pp. 764–767.

20. Also see section 172 of the Gerichtsverfassungsgesetz (Constitution of the Courts Act), which provides for the exclusion of the public from a hearing if commercial, personal, or industrial interests would be violated by disclosure of information.

21. H. von Huelsen, "Kanadische und europäische Reaktionen auf die U.S. pretrial discovery und die internationale Rechtshilfe," 9 *Recht der internationalen Wirtschaft* 546 (1982). Also see Avenarius, *Kleines Rechtswörterbuch* (Freiburg im Breisgau: Verlag Herder, 1985), for brief discussions of the concepts of *Rechtsstaatlichkeit* (rule of law) and *Verhältnismässigkeit* (proportionality).

22. Meessen had authored a legal opinion in support of the German government position—"The Taking Of Evidence From, Not In, A Foreign State"—in its amicus brief in *Anschütz*. This opinion was appended to that brief and has been reprinted at 25 *I.L.M.* 832 (1986).

23. Both drafts and their accompanying commentaries have been reproduced in *Vorschläge zum Erlass einer Urkundenvorlageverordnung,* Claus-Dieter Brandt, ed. (privately printed, 1987). Informal English translations have been made, but the translations herein are the author's. All references to the drafts and their commentaries refer to the pagination of this booklet. Later revisions of a minor nature were made in November 1987 but were not received in time for incorporation herein.

24. Meessen, "The Taking of Evidence," pp. 46, 47. Also see Article 9 of the Hague Evidence Convention.

25. See Article 1 of both drafts.

26. Meessen, "The Taking of Evidence," p. 46.

27. Ibid., p. 49.

28. Meessen, "The Taking of Evidence," pp. 49, 73.

29. Industry draft, Article 3(2). See article 9 of the BMJ draft, which permits the court to impose sanctions provided for in ZPO section 380 against a third person. That section concerns sanctions against a witness who fails to appear at a hearing, but the BMJ drafters feel that because document production plays as important a role in U.S procedure as witness testimony does in German, the witness sanctions should be applied analogously to third persons for the purpose of the regulation. Of course, Meessen finds this to be an unacceptable deviation from fundamental German procedural principles. Meessen, ibid., p. 47.

30. Meessen, ibid., p. 68.

31. Ibid., p. 59.

32. BMJ commentary, p. 9.

33. Meessen, "The Taking of Evidence," p. 52.

34. Industry draft, Article 3(2).

9

Dealing with Dealing: Plea Bargaining in the Federal Republic of Germany

Dennis P. McLaughlin

Plea bargaining has come to West Germany. So far it exists only in the shadows of formal West German criminal procedure and is only beginning to be analyzed and discussed openly by legal scholars, prosecutors, defense lawyers, and judges. Even for many who are active within the West German criminal justice system, plea bargaining remains, due to their limited contact with it, a mysterious and somewhat terrifying creature, only heard about and rarely observed.

There is no doubt that the necessity and permissible limits of plea bargaining are extremely explosive issues within the West German legal community. The debate about it will certainly intensify in the next few years and promises to be one of the most significant debates for West German criminal procedure since the original adoption of the nationwide Code of Criminal Procedure in 1871. In fact, the possibility of significant amendments to that code, which still exists in large part as originally formulated, is one of the crucial plea bargaining issues to be faced by those who work in German criminal justice.

This chapter does not take any position on whether West Germany should formally adopt plea bargaining into its criminal procedure. Nor does this discussion purport to provide either philosophical or procedural solutions to the growing debate about plea bargaining's utility and desirability in West Germany. The article simply presents some thoughts, from a U.S. prosecutor who has seen both criminal justice systems, on three areas of potential interest in West Germany's present plea bargaining debate: (1) Why does plea bargaining exist in the United States, specifically Arizona, and why is it now appearing in West Germany, which has until recently successfully done without it? (2) How is plea bargaining carried out in West Germany? (3) What problems will West Germany face if it attempts to formally accept plea bargaining into its criminal procedure?

Obviously, these questions cannot be treated exhaustively in one short chapter. But the discussion that follows will provide some insights to those in the United States who are interested in the West German problem and especially to those in West Germany who, in the next few years, will have to decide whether and to what extent plea bargaining should have a place in West German criminal procedure.

Plea Bargaining

A plea bargain is an agreement between a criminal defendant and the state that the defendant will plead guilty to a certain charge or charges and forego full trial and that in return the state will grant the defendant a benefit or benefits concerning the charge(s) and/or the sentence on the charge(s). Until approximately twenty years ago, plea bargaining's history in the United States was similar to the present situation in West Germany. Plea bargaining existed (and undoubtedly to a far greater extent than it presently does in West Germany), but it was carried on behind closed doors, subject to no formal procedural regulation or safeguards. This began to change in the 1960s and 1970s, when plea bargaining came into the open and was regulated statutorily. Between 70 and 90 percent of U.S. criminal cases are now settled each year by plea bargaining. At least one commentator put the figure even higher,[1] and it may be in certain jurisdictions. Plea bargaining is now as much a part of formal criminal procedure in the United States as trial by jury. In Arizona, for example, rules concerning plea bargaining have been formally incorporated into the Arizona Rules of Criminal Procedure.[2]

The Situation in Arizona

Why does plea bargaining exist in the United States to the extent that it does? With respect to the state of Arizona, one can identify four interrelated "forces" that drive the plea bargaining system.

Too many cases, too few courts and prosecutors. In the state of Arizona, as in most of the United States, crime rates are high for felonies, defined as those crimes for which a defendant may be sentenced to the state prison, and for misdemeanors, such as shoplifting and drunken driving. At the state level, where the lion's share of crime is prosecuted and judged, courts and prosecuting agencies are understaffed. If every case where a defendant has a *right* to trial were actually to go to full trial under these circumstances, the system would almost certainly collapse.

Lack of nontrial disposition alternatives for prosecutors. Arizona's criminal procedure system does not allow for nontrial disposition other than by plea bargaining. Assuming that the evidence of the crime is sufficient and the victim is willing to prosecute, the Arizona prosecutor has no realistic alternative to taking the particular case to trial or to plea bargaining. The only exceptions, relatively few and far between, are cases involving drug possession where prosecution can be suspended and later dismissed if the defendant successfully completes pretrial probation involving drug counseling. In other types of cases where there are no factual or legal problems, plea bargaining is the sole nontrial disposition method open to the prosecutor.

A cumbersome and time-consuming trial procedure. Jury trial, required in felony cases and in many misdemeanor cases (including, most importantly, drunk driving cases), is a very complex process. Choosing the jury can, by itself, last days or weeks in important cases. Even in a normal case, the process will last a half-day, which is longer than many complete German criminal trials. The rules of evidence are more formal than in West Germany. Issues such as the admissibility of breath test results in drunk driving cases, the legality of search and seizure, the suggestivity and reliability of an identification procedure, and the admissibility of prior convictions and confessions are of constitutional dimension. Their litigation requires large expenditures of time and effort.

The person on whom most of this work falls is the prosecutor. In contrast to his German colleague, a U.S. prosecutor's major efforts on a particular case first begin after the charge is filed. Trials in the United States are an adversary process, wherein the parties present all of their own evidence and cross-examine the other side's witnesses. Unlike West Germany, the judge is not responsible for taking evidence. The prosecutor bears the burden of proving the defendant's guilt beyond a reasonable doubt. Before trial, he (or she) must organize his evidence, disclose it to defense counsel, subpoena and interview the witnesses whom he will call, interview defense witnesses and review defense evidence. He must do all of this while still covering court calendars and doing administrative tasks.

At trial, the prosecutor must pick the jury, make an opening statement describing the state's case to the jury, present all of his evidence, cross-examine defense witnesses, present closing arguments to the jury, submit and argue jury instructions, respond to defense motions and arguments throughout trial, and finally wait out the verdict. It is a physically and emotionally stressful process, so that going to trial more than once or twice a month is rare. After all this, as all prosecutors know, one can never be certain that the jury will convict.

A plea bargain, on the other hand, assures conviction and punishment of the defendant. Witnesses and victims need not be put through the ordeal of testifying. Appeals by the defendant are preempted. Court and prosecutor time is saved. The psychological pressure for certainty of this kind is almost impossible to resist in those cases where a solid plea bargain can be achieved.

A sentencing system that encourages criminal defendants to plea bargain. So far, all of the reasons stated make plea bargaining attractive to courts and prosecutors. Why, however, are defendants willing to go along with this system? The reason is Arizona's sentencing system.

In 1978, the Arizona legislature amended the penal code and established a new system of felony sentencing. The system limits the discretion of judges in sentencing in felony cases by statutorily fixing minimum, presumptive ("normal"), and maximum sentences for all felony offenses. The sentences are fixed for a felony depending on its "type" (sexual crimes against children, felonies using weapons or where serious injury results, all other felonies), its statutorily defined "class" (ranging from Class 6, the least serious felonies, to Class 1, first-degree murder), and whether it is the defendant's first, second, or third conviction. Judges may deviate within the range of minimum and maximum, but they must state reasons for doing so on the record, which may be reviewed by an appellate court. Offenses committed using weapons, while the defendant was on probation or parole or out on bail, or under other specified conditions are punished still more heavily under statutes that, in addition, often specify how much of the sentence a defendant must serve before becoming eligible for parole. Under certain circumstances, defendants will be required to serve out their whole sentence and may not receive parole at all.

The end result is that a large percentage of defendants face the threat of very long sentences if they go to trial and are convicted by the jury. This is particularly true if they have prior convictions, used a weapon, or committed the crime under one or more of the other specified conditions that require a heavier sentence. Accordingly, most defendants are willing to accept a plea bargain that offers a stipulation by the state to lighter punishment. The sentencing system, therefore, balances the other three factors by providing the defendant as well as the state with a reason to plea bargain.

Naturally, the sentencing system is not so harsh in all cases, and not every defendant will face the possibility of harsh punishment. For example, probation is often available for first offenders, depending on the crime. Such cases are generally handled by a plea to a reduced charge and a stipulation to probation by the state.

The Arizona sentencing system, flexible for first offenders but harsh toward repeat offenders, gives both prosecutors and defendants an incentive to plea bargain. The system's fixed framework also provides both parties with a yardstick against which to measure the risks and benefits of a proposed plea bargain. The sentencing system is what allows balanced plea bargains, acceptable to both parties, to be struck.

It should be noted that the four forces just discussed do not exist in isolation. In practice, they reinforce each other, thus making plea bargaining the method of disposition in the vast majority of Arizona criminal cases.

The Situation in West Germany

In comparison, plea bargaining has never previously existed in West Germany because it has never previously been necessary. The rates of comparable crimes are often significantly lower in West Germany than in the United States,[3] although such comparisons must be treated with caution. Moreover, many offenses (particularly property crimes such as theft) that may be classified as misdemeanors or felonies in the United States, depending on the circumstances, are misdemeanors in West Germany. For example, approximately three-fourths of all West Germans charged with criminal offenses in 1980 were charged with either driving while intoxicated or property crimes such as theft, both of which are misdemeanors under West German law.[4] The fact that a crime is a misdemeanor has important consequences with respect to the availability of nontrial disposition methods.

In felony cases, where an investigation produces sufficient evidence to justify a charge against a particular individual, the prosecutor must file that charge and proceed to trial on it.[5] But where the offense is a misdemeanor, the prosecutor can choose not to prosecute if the defendant's actual offense is minor and there is no public interest served by prosecution.[6] Alternatively, the prosecutor can agree to no further prosecution of a misdemeanor in return for the defendant's meeting certain conditions, which can include payment of restitution or a fine.[7] If the case is within the jurisdiction of the lowest criminal courts and the sole sentence sought is a fine, a third possibility is the submission of a proposed penal order (*Strafbefehl*) by the prosecutor to the judge. The penal order sets forth the fine sought by the prosecutor. If the penal order is accepted by the judge, and not objected to by the defendant within one week of receipt, it becomes the final judgment, and no trial is necessary in that case.[8] Because fines are used much more extensively in West Germany,[9] even in cases where a U.S. court would not feel that a fine was adequate, a large percentage of cases are handled by the penal order process.

Where a misdemeanor charge is based on violations of administrative regulations, it can be referred to the appropriate administrative agency for handling. Certain other very minor misdemeanors, such as fights between drunken bar patrons or neighbors, can be referred to the victim to prosecute on his or her own, where the state prosecutor finds no significant public interest in prosecution.[10] The state prosecutor need not deal with the case further, and the court will often dismiss the case as insignificant. Finally, if in the judgment of the prosecutor the sentence for a particular charge, whether misdemeanor or felony, will not affect a previously imposed sentence on other charges or a pending sentence on other charges, then that charge need not be prosecuted.[11]

To see the results of the whole system of nontrial options, one need only look at the statistics concerning state prosecutor's offices at the *Landgericht* level (effectively the trial-level prosecutor's offices) in the state of Baden-Württemberg in 1985.[12] The total number of cases handled in 1985 was 644,125. Of this total, 284,288 cases could not be prosecuted because the identity of the suspected perpetrator never became known. Of the remaining 359,837 cases processed, 22 percent were not pursued because of insufficient evidence of guilt to charge the suspect.[13] More than 20 percent were not prosecuted pursuant to the minor guilt/no public interest statute[14] or pursuant to an agreement to pay restitution, pay a fine, or meet other conditions.[15] More than 9 percent were handled by referring them back to the victim or to administrative authorities. Out of almost 360,000 cases, charges were actually submitted to a court for trial in only 15 percent.

The distribution of work among the courts also shows that the West German court system is designed to free the higher courts for trial of more serious cases. The *Amtsgerichte*, the lowest West German criminal courts, handled almost 1.5 million criminal cases in 1984.[16] The other main trial-level courts, the higher-level *Landgerichte*, handled approximately 13,000 criminal cases in the same year.[17] Of the total of 50,753 cases submitted for trial by the state prosecutor's offices in Baden-Württemberg, all but 1,183 were handled by the *Amtsgerichte*.[18] Furthermore, more than 80 percent of the cases at the *Amtsgericht* level were triable before a single judge, rather than a panel of one judge and two lay jurors, thus saving both time and money and resulting in speedier disposition.[19]

Given the nontrial disposition methods and court organization that exist in West Germany, it is no wonder that plea bargaining has traditionally been unknown. An enormous percentage of minor cases are processed without the need for lengthy court proceedings, thereby leaving the higher courts free to focus their full attention on the small fraction of more serious cases that actually require a full trial.

When a case is of a serious nature and goes to trial, West Germany's normally efficient trial procedure usually obviates the need for any plea bargaining. I have personally watched a West German court finish, in one day, the trials of four cases, each of which would have required a felony trial lasting at least three court days in the United States. The fact that approximately 40 percent of criminal defendants confess at trial[20] certainly helps to speed up certain cases. But the procedure itself is also simply faster than its U.S. counterpart.

Because West German lay jurors sit for all cases in their particular court on their day of service, there is no need for lengthy questioning of the proposed jury panel, as exists in the United States. Because the panel has both lay jurors and professional judges on it, jury instructions at the end of the case are also unnecessary. There are no opening statements by the attorneys. The rules of evidence and in-court procedure are, with certain exceptions, more flexible than those in the United States. Narrative answers by witnesses are permissible; the first question generally asked of a witness is to tell what he or she knows about the case. If the defendant is willing to speak on the case after being informed of his or her right to remain silent, he or she becomes the first witness. If he or she makes a full confession, the trial is over. Even statements short of full confession limit the issues and measurably shorten the trial's evidence-taking phase. A German trial also determines both guilt and sentencing issues in one proceeding, saving a significant amount of court time. Because the defendant's prior criminal record is always relevant to sentencing, it can be read at the end of the evidence-taking phase of the trial. Confessions, identification, and search and seizure are rarely if ever at issue in German courts. An exclusionary rule for evidence is unknown in German courts except for a ban on diaries or secret tape-recordings. The judge is responsible for establishing the facts and can ask leading questions. Taken together, all of these factors produce a significantly faster trial in most types of cases.

The West German sentencing system also does not encourage defendants to plea bargain because it does not threaten them with statutorily fixed harsh penalties if they are convicted at trial. The West German sentencing system is, from an Arizona perspective, relatively "defendant friendly." The much more extensive use of fines has already been mentioned.[21] Penalites are, for the most part, significantly lighter than for comparable crimes in Arizona, both with respect to the statutorily fixed upper and lower limits and the sentences actually handed down.[22] Except for murder, which is punishable by "life imprisonment" (defined as twenty-five years, with the sentence subject to review after fifteen years), the maximum sentence for any crime in West Germany is fifteen years. Because the penal code sets only upper and lower limits, judges have relatively broad discretion. Statistically, sentences exceeding one year are rare and are reserved for more serious cases.[23]

There is also general agreement that confessions at trial in West Germany are rewarded with milder sentences. The official reason is that a confession shows contrition; the unofficial reason is that it saves the state money and court time. Thus, the dynamics of the West German trial and sentencing system do not encourage plea bargaining; they simply encourage a certain percentage of defendants to confess at trial.

In summary, none of the four factors that drive the plea bargaining system in Arizona has existed in West Germany. The higher-level courts have handled their small fraction of criminal cases efficiently using normal trial procedure, whereas the lower courts have had nontrial methods available to clear up their large volume of cases.

Why, then, has plea bargaining of a type recognizable to a U.S. prosecutor begun to appear in West Germany, and why is it creating such alarm? The answers to these two questions are (1) because plea bargaining has become indispensable in certain cases and (2) because in its present form it represents a serious challenge to the philosophy and established practices of the West German criminal justice system.

Recent amendments to the FRG's narcotics laws now permit West German trial courts to take into account the defendant's cooperation after arrest when fixing sentence after a narcotics trial.[24] The legislative authorization in narcotics cases came about because of the West German legislature's belief that lighter punishment in less important cases was a reasonable price to pay for more effective enforcement of the narcotics laws. The authorization did not open up a bona fide plea bargaining process, however, because it was really nothing more than a sentence mitigation statute to be used *by the judge* after an otherwise "normal" criminal trial.

In the field of white-collar crime, however, full-fledged plea bargaining is now occurring without legislative authorization through the collaboration of judges, prosecutors, and defense attorneys. The reason for that is the inability of the West German criminal justice system to efficiently handle white-collar cases, whether by nontrial disposition methods or trial. Although complicated white-collar crimes make up only a tiny fraction of all prosecuted crimes, they require a wholly disproportionate amount of West German court and prosecutor time. They can take years for the state prosecutors to investigate and charge and months or years for the courts to try. The evidence is often extremely complex, involving expert testimony and literally hundreds of volumes of documents. The result for understaffed prosecutors and courts is the same as if the crime rates had suddenly exploded. Because so much time must be devoted to these cases, the system quickly becomes clogged as the never-ending old cases compete with new cases for court and prosecutor time. A court trying a white-collar case may have to deal with that case exclusively for months or years and is effectively unavailable for other cases.

Moreover, none of the normal methods of nontrial disposition is justifiable in these cases. Even where the crimes are technically mis-demeanors, prosecutors cannot simply ignore years of knowing activity and illegal profits and claim that (1) the defendant's actions involve a low level of guilt and the public interest does not require prosecution; or (2) restitution and a fine in return for no further prosecution represent an appropriate disposition. Penal orders are also not available because crimes are rarely within the jurisdiction of the lowest criminal courts and, in any case, fines are not deemed a sufficient penalty. The only remaining method of disposition is trial.

The normally efficient West German trial procedure, however, is not well adapted to processing these cases. Due to the voluminous and complex evidence that must be presented, trials drag on and on. The required reading of documents in open court alone can take weeks or months of court time. Confessions are also rare because reputations and huge amounts of money are at issue, and relatively severe punishments can be expected upon conviction. White-collar defendants, understand-ably, wait to see if the state really has the evidence to prove their guilt. Only then do they consider confessing in return for leniency guaranteed by the prosecutor and court.

Given this state of affairs, it is no surprise that plea bargaining has been used in an increasing number of complex white-collar cases, as courts and prosecutors, in particular, seek "unorthodox" methods of solving the problems posed by them. It is also noteworthy that the four Arizona factors previously discussed explain the relative leniency toward the white-collar defendant observable in most West German plea bargains. Because the first three "state motivating" factors (court and prosecutor overload, lack of nontrial disposition alternatives, and cumbersome trial procedure) manifest themselves in white-collar cases and because the fourth "defendant motivating" factor (longer sentences in the event of trial and conviction) is not present to stimulate defendant participation, one would expect to see plea bargains whose terms favor the white-collar defendant. Because only the state has a real incentive to plea bargain, the defendant need only agree when a very good plea bargain is being offered. That is exactly what usually happens. Defendants often receive suspended sentences and probation in return for restitution in crimes involving enormous losses and years of criminal activity. This fact angers many in the justice system and among the general public who see a system developing in which defendants rich from illegal profits purchase a more favorable outcome in their trials at little cost to themselves.

How Plea Bargaining Operates

There are as yet no fixed mechanisms for West German plea agreements because it is a new phenomenon, does not exist officially, and is obviously not statutorily required. Nevertheless, certain common characteristics can be described.[25]

Plea bargaining presently occurs almost exclusively in white-collar crime cases.[26] It is extremely rare in cases involving violent crime or political crime. Although it does not occur in every white-collar case and it does take different forms, it is now almost an everyday occurrence for prosecutors involved in economic crime litigation. German plea bargains generally involve a defendant's agreement not to make motions for the taking of evidence (resulting in a faster trial and disposition)[27] or agreement to confess some or all of his or her activities. The state may guarantee (1) a suspended sentence and probation; (2) a milder sentence on certain counts and/or a milder total sentence; or (3) no further prosecution of the case if full restitution is made or other conditions are met.[28]

Judges in white-collar cases almost always take part in the negotiation of plea agreements. Bargaining and agreement in some cases take place at the time for setting the trial date, when the court meets with the parties to figure out how long the case will take to try. Bargaining can also occur after the beginning of the trial, when both parties have had an opportunity to see the actual evidence and judge the probabilities. The prosecutor, court, and defense discuss the evidence and come to an agreement acceptable to all sides. Usually, the prosecutor will dismiss certain counts as not affecting sentence,[29] and/or informally agree to a particular sentence recommendation in return for a confession on the remaining counts by the defendant or a waiver of further motions that would delay verdict and judgment on those remaining counts or both. Lay jurors sitting for the trial often know nothing of what has been worked out in advance of the trial or during the breaks in ongoing proceedings.

Future Problems

Plea bargaining in West Germany is a relatively new and still limited phenomenon. Yet it is already sparking the same types of criticism it has long known in the United States, albeit with little effect on its continued use. In both countries, plea bargaining is perceived as an admission that the criminal justice system, from the standpoint of both organization and resources, is inadequate. The basic ideals of a full and fair trial of each case and of no deals with criminals apparently appeal to the West German populace just as much as they do to the people of the United States.

As previously discussed, the West German system, even without plea bargaining, has used nontrial dispositions of various types to handle a huge percentage of all criminal cases. Therefore, any belief on the part of the West German population that trial is the statistically "normal" means of disposition in all criminal cases long ago lost any rational basis. But the West German populace could be confident, until very recently, that the criminal procedure system was at least handling more serious crimes via full trial. That this confidence may no longer be justified, and that the system may be breaking down under the strain of white-collar crimes and other types of criminal cases, justifiably concerns those working in West Germany's criminal justice system.

Finding a solution to fix the breakdown will not be easy. An increase in resources and personnel for police, courts, and prosecuting agencies is no more likely, in and of itself, to solve the problem in West Germany as it would in the United States. Therefore, procedural changes appear to be the only feasible alternative. Yet procedural changes must either modify the traditional German trial system to allow speedier disposition of the "problem" cases or provide some as-yet-undesigned alternative that eliminates the need for trial in those cases altogether. Neither possibility promises to be painless or particularly satisfying to West Germans. Innovation and change are always somewhat slower in tradition-loving West Germany, even when the benefits are obvious to all. Such benefits would hardly be obvious to all where plea bargaining or possible modification of long-existing trial procedures was at issue.

Leaving aside the West German public's distaste for and distrust of plea bargaining, there is little likelihood that it can be formally adopted into West German criminal procedure any time soon. For the criminal justice community, formalization of plea bargaining will involve clearing three hurdles: (1) developing a formal procedure; (2) determining when the system should be available and how it should function to dispose of the targeted cases fairly and efficiently; (3) harmonizing plea bargaining with the philosophy and traditions of West German justice.

The procedural hurdle would almost certainly be the easiest to clear. Plea bargaining would need to be statutorily authorized and regulated, and the participation of courts and prosecutors specifically would have to be authorized, with limits on their activities also fixed. A procedure for actually taking pleas would need to be devised. A system somewhat similar to that used in the United States might be the answer.

Many of the procedural objections raised against plea bargaining by West German commentators stem from the fact that it currently takes place in the context of the criminal trial itself and involves the very judge who must impartially weigh the evidence if no bargain can be reached. Because the trial is the only formal court proceeding known to German criminal procedure after the prosecutor submits charges and the court has reviewed the submitted charges for sufficiency, such a dual role for judges is justifiably criticized as unfair to both judge and defendant.

This problem might disappear, however, if a formal plea proceeding were available, separate from the trial and handled by an organizationally and functionally separate "plea chamber" at each court. The plea chamber could be assigned the duty of handling plea bargains, whether proposed prior to trial or during the proceedings.

If a formal proceeding and forum for plea bargains existed, the trial judge could concentrate on his or her present duties under West German criminal procedure: (1) investigating the facts and law relating to a charged offense through taking evidence at trial; and (2) deciding on guilt and the appropriate sentence based on the result of that trial. He or she would not need to fear "contamination" of neutrality before or during the trial through participation in plea discussions because any such discussions would take place before a different judge in the plea chamber. The dilemma created by having trial judges participate in plea discussions, and the problem of trial judges being challenged for bias when plea bargains fall through, would be eliminated.

Individual plea chambers could be connected organizationally to a particular trial court or courts, with cases automatically assigned to each in parallel. Thus, the requirement under West German law that the jurisdiction of judges must be fixed in advance of a particular case would not be violated. Pleas could be taken by a single judge (as in the United States), or lay jurors could also be included on the plea panels. Either alternative would eliminate the problem under the present system of plea bargains being reached at trial without the participation or knowledge of lay jurors. If the law permitted a plea to be taken by a single judge, but trial jurisdiction normally lay with a panel, then in cases where no sentence was specified in the agreement, the case could be sent to a regular trial chamber for trial concerning sentence only. All proceedings of the plea chambers could be publicly noticed and open to the public, exactly like a trial chamber.

Opponents of plea bargaining claim that West German prosecutors are forbidden to engage in it by the legality principle,[30] which requires them to fully investigate all facts surrounding an alleged crime and to charge the crime or crimes supported by the evidence discovered. Critics also argue that plea bargaining amounts to a violation of the legality principle because it involves the acceptance by prosecutors of guilty pleas to charges less serious than those with which the defendant was charged and for which he or she could be convicted at trial. (An example, using U.S. crimes for illustration, would be a case in which the evidence was sufficient to convict for armed robbery but the prosecutor accepted a plea to the lesser charge of robbery.)

The claim that the legality principle forbids all plea bargaining is certainly too broad. It appears to be at least partly based on the mistaken assumption that "charge bargaining" (reducing an individual charge to a lower charge despite facts justifying the higher charge) would be the only option for West German prosecutors. Assuming that the critics' analysis is correct, charge bargaining could probably be forbidden without seriously hampering the operation of a formal plea bargaining system, so long as other methods, such as dismissal of certain charges[31] or agreements concerning sentencing, were authorized. Dismissal is already authorized where it will not affect sentencing, and it is hard to argue that the legality principle extends to agreements concerning sentencing on a particular charge. Moreover, the legality principle is hardly the monolith it once was. As previously discussed, the Code of Criminal Procedure already makes it inapplicable to many misdemeanors, which are handled by various methods of nontrial disposition or dismissal.

The second hurdle in the formalization of plea bargaining will be deciding when it should be available and how it should be designed to dispose of targeted cases. If plea bargaining is adopted in all types of cases, despite being "necessary" in only certain types, such as white-collar cases, there is a risk of disturbing mechanisms that have smoothly handled "nonproblem" cases heretofore. On the other hand, making plea bargaining available only in certain types of cases opens the way for an equal protection challenge by defendants charged with offenses for which plea bargaining is not available. Their argument would be that either all defendants must have theoretical access to the plea bargaining system (although without automatic right to a plea bargain in every case) or no defendants must have access. Moreover, a distinction among types of cases may confirm public suspicions that plea bargaining is only an option for well-educated, well-off defendants who engage in large-scale fraud, embezzlement, or similar crimes.

Reconciling plea bargaining with traditional German legal philosophy and principles will be the highest hurdle of all. The crux of West Germany's aversion to plea bargaining is not based on objections to a particular procedure or system. It is philosophical. Although the concept of trial in all cases is as much a myth in West Germany as in the United States, a plea bargaining system conflicts with the West German jurisprudential ideal. According to this ideal, truth determination is best served by a full trial at which all facts are explored by the trier of fact, after which a just decision on guilt or innocence and on an appropriate sentence is reached. Judges are the key figures in the actual process and in the ideal. They are traditionally supposed to fix sentences on the basis of full trial and to have full discretion in doing so. Deciding on conviction or sentence by way of plea bargaining brings unwanted parties into this process and limits the judge's ability and discretion to do his or her job properly and legally. Plea bargaining's negotiating aspects also conflict with the West German view that judges and state prosecutors are not negotiators or advocates; they are servants of justice and finders of truth.

It is clear that although the present system of plea bargaining is hardly satisfactory, least of all to the German public, formal incorporation of plea bargaining will also bring enormous problems. The basic question becomes, How can a system to which such bargaining is so foreign suddenly incorporate it formally? Yet, if it does not incorporate and regulate plea bargaining, how can the criminal justice system continue to endure it without risking a loss of public confidence in the essential fairness of the system?

In the coming years, West Germany's criminal justice community must attempt to reconcile actual practice and basic ideals, never an enviable task. Any changes must either harmonize with traditional legal philosophy and principle, or the philosophy and principles must undergo modification. Both alternatives will present an intellectual challenge of the greatest magnitude and will encounter resistance from all quarters. Only time will tell whether West Germany is capable of "dealing with dealing" by formally accepting it and regulating it.

Notes

1. Langbein, "Land Without Plea Bargaining: How the Germans Do It," 78 *Michigan Law Review* 220 (1979).

2. Rule 17, Arizona Rules of Criminal Procedure.

3. Langbein, "Land Without Plea Bargaining," pp. 209–210.

4. T. Weigend, "Sentencing in West Germany," 42 *Maryland Law Review* 48, n. 56 (1983).

5. Section 152(II), Strafprozessordnung (hereinafter StPO). This is the so-called *Legalitätsprinzip*, or legality principle, a rule of compulsory prosecution. The legality principle is actually intended to protect the West German citizen

by removing the possibility of arbitrary prosecutorial oppression or favoritism in particular cases.

6. StPO, section 153.

7. StPO, section 153a.

8. StPO, Sections 407–412.

9. Weigend, "Sentencing," pp. 47–48.

10. StPO, sections 374–394.

11. StPO, sections 154, 154a.

12. "Die Justiz," *Amtsblatt des Justizministeriums Baden-Württemberg*, Jahrgang 35, no. 10 (October 1986), p. 400.

13. StPO, section 170(II).

14. StPO, section 153.

15. StPO, section 153a.

16. Statistisches Bundesamt, *Ausgewählte Zahlen für die Rechtspflege*, Fachserie 10 (1984), line 1.

17. Ibid.

18. "Die Justiz."

19. Ibid.

20. Conversations with prosecutors at the State Prosecutor's Office, Stuttgart. See also Langbein, "Land Without Plea Bargaining," p. 218.

21. Weigend, "Sentencing," pp. 47–49.

22. Ibid.

23. Ibid. It should be noted, however, that the vast majority of West German defendants will serve two-thirds of their sentences before parole is possible, whereas the actual time served in Arizona depends on the particular crime, defendant, and sentencing statutes involved and may vary from a small fraction of the sentence to the entire mandated sentence.

24. Paragraph 31 of the Narcotics Law (*Betäubungsmittelgesetz*) gives trial courts discretion to impose milder punishment or no punishment at all where a defendant has cooperated in the investigation of past narcotics offenses or in the prevention of planned offenses.

25. Where not otherwise noted, this section is a product of conversations with prosecutors in the Economic Crimes Division of the State Prosecutor's Office, Stuttgart.

26. R. Hassemer and G. Hippler, "Informelle Absprachen in der Praxis des deutschen Strafverfahrens," *Strafverteidiger*, Jahrgang 6, Heft 8 (August 1986), pp. 360–363.

27. StPO, section 244.

28. StPO, section 153a.

29. StPO, sections 154, 154a.

30. See note 5.

31. StPO, sections 154, 154a.

The German Political Scene After Reykjavik

Theo Sommer
Editor in Chief, *Die Zeit*

Helmut Schmidt was once asked to characterize the nature of German politics and to describe the chancellor's job. By way of an answer, he told the story of a New York taxi driver who was driving behind a truck. At each red light, when the truck stopped, the truck driver would jump out, take a big wooden beam, and bang it against the side of the truck. The truck driver did this four or five times. The fifth time the taxi driver got out and said, "Now listen, I've been watching you. Could you explain to me what you are doing?" The truck driver responded. "It's quite simple! I'm driving a two and a half ton truck and I've got a three and a half ton load of parrots. To get anywhere, I have to keep one ton of them in the air all the time." That, according to Schmidt, is the job of the chancellor—to keep one ton of the parrots in the air all the time! (I think Chancellor Helmut Kohl would not feel much differently. Politics is a messy process that is often hard to understand, and it is of course dangerous for anyone to try his hand at predictions.) At this point, I would like to make a few statements about German politics, then give you my assessment of the election prospects, and in the end perhaps turn my attention to some of the foreign policy problems with which Germans are grappling.

This speech was given to the Annual Conference of the Robert Bosch Foundation Alumni Association, December 6, 1986, Washington, D.C. Introductory remarks were made by Ambassador Günther van Well, Federal Republic of Germany.

The West German Domestic Situation:
Normal, Stable, Reliable, Prosperous

The first thesis I would like to put forward is that West Germany is a *normal* country. It need not give anyone goose pimples. We have our share of acute problems, but none is specific to West Germany. Rather, they stem from the predicament in which all the advanced industrial democracies find themselves.

Second, I think it is worth making the point that Germany is a *stable* country. Our institutions have passed the test of time. We have managed two *Machtwechsel*, two "changeovers," one in 1969 and one in 1982. The system was not shaken; it took the changeovers very well. The consensus between the government parties and the opposition parties is far greater than the agitated rhetoric of the election campaign appears to suggest. The center still holds between them. The Christian Democratic Union (CDU), the Christian Social Union (CSU), and the Free Democratic Party (FDP) polled 56 percent last month (November 1986). The opposition Social Democratic Party (SPD) was not exactly routed; it still polled 38 percent. I think the system proved its openness by admitting new forces, such as the Greens, which polled 7 percent at the time. Furthermore, there is no such thing as "ungovernability." There was none in 1983, and I do not think ungovernability will be a problem we will face after January 25, 1987.

In its often bumbling and rumbling way, the system works. As Brigitte Bardot once said about *l'erotisme*—it is not the problem; it is the solution. I think that not even the Hamburg predicament—where neither of the two camps, the CDU on the one hand together with the FDP, and the Social Democrats and the Greens on the other hand, can muster a majority—is a threat to that system. There is always the possibility of forming a grand coalition, and I think this is going to happen, either overtly or covertly. Either covertly or overtly, I think we will have a grand coalition, and I think that if worse came to worst in Bonn, that would be the way out and no one need worry about ungovernability.

My third thesis is that Germany is a *reliable* country. There is a lot of talk about the *Wende*, a "turnabout" or even a "U-turn," in German affairs. But during the past four years (1982–1986) Chancellor Kohl has discovered that big countries are like supertankers: You cannot turn them around on the spot. At best, you can veer off the previous course by a few degrees, thereby setting a direction that eventually will lead you to a different destination. But there is bound to be more continuity than change, and there has been more continuity than change during these past four years. This is especially true in the field of foreign policy.

National interest, national perception, and national emotions do not change that easily.

This is particularly obvious in the field of foreign policy. It holds true for economic and social policies as well. Kohl is neither Ronald Reagan nor Margaret Thatcher. He tightened the social net before it was torn by the sheer weight of inflated benefit programs, yet he would slash the excrescences rather than kill the system itself. Any objective observer will have to admit that we have been "over-egging the pudding," as the British put it. There was a lot of facetious talk about truffled gooseliver paid by the free medical health service before the excesses were cut out. But there is still free medical health service, and there is no dismantling of the welfare state. It is not by accident that we talk about *soziale Marktwirtschaft* (social market economy) where others may prefer the term *free enterprise*. Nor is it by happenstance that the budget of the Sozialministerium is bigger than the defense budget.

The welfare state, which the Christian Democrats after all were instrumental in creating, is not only a matter of entitlements. Social security—taking care of the weak and the needy—is part and parcel of overall security. This could not be otherwise in a divided country situated on the western border of the Communist colossus. The social net has stood us in good stead. First, we weathered price inflation, and now protracted unemployment, without disruption to the political system. There has not been any radicalization either on the Left or on the Right, and there has not been any societal dislocation. These are the positive effects of the *soziale Marktwirtschaft*.

Reliability also characterizes our attitude toward rights. We have not turned our backs on the liberal traditions of our constitution with regard to terrorism, that scourge of the modern age, or with regard to those among the needy, the laden, and the persecuted of the world who ask for asylum. In fact, given what other neighboring countries—Italy, France, Denmark, and Sweden—have been doing in these fields recently, we can be quite proud of our record. Of course, we have to combat terrorism, although I sometimes wonder whether it is such a central issue as the newspaper headlines suggest. Of course, we cannot absorb millions of Turks or Sri Lankans or Chinese. The point is, however, that so far we have suffered some afflictions, but we have stood fast by our principles.

Fourth, Germany is a *prosperous* country. I mean this in the very broad sense of the term. Orderly, clean; no poverty strikes the eye as it does in so many other countries, including some regions of this country. But I mean it also in the narrow sense of the term. Chancellor Kohl was lucky; he became chancellor when there was a worldwide economic upturn, especially in the United States, and when the oil price dropped from $34 to about $12 a barrel (now $14 or $15). Chancellor Kohl has been the most immediate beneficiary of both developments. This is probably the most important factor determining the outcome of the elections. All other factors are dwarfed into nothingness by this.

West Germany's gross national product (GNP) last year (1985) amounted to more than DM 1.8 trillion, our per capita income to more than DM 30,000. Inflation went down to less than zero (economists for some reason are never able to fathom all this negative inflation). Growth figures have been improving. Again we had minus growth of 1 to 1.5 percent in 1982, then a positive growth of at least 3 percent in the course of these past few years. Productivity has gone up; it stands at about 3 percent.

This signals the end of what Ambassador Richard Burt used to call "Eurosclerosis." In fact, there are many more Europeans nowadays who talk about "American sclerosis" when looking at the productivity figures and the trade deficits of that country. The mood has changed. Perhaps the facts have not changed to the same extent that the mood has changed, but the mood definitely has altered. Federal borrowing is down from almost DM 50 billion a year to DM 22 billion. We have been amassing a current account surplus since 1983. It will approach about DM 70 billion this year (1986), which is good in one respect and bad in another respect; it puts us on the dock right next to the Japanese.

There is one factor that mars this rather positive picture: unemployment. Depending on the season of the year, unemployment hovers between 8 percent and 10 percent, affecting between 2 and 2.5 million people. It has not so far created any political problems, which is astounding because Hitler was brought to power by unemployment in 1933. There seems to be more societal tolerance for unemployment now than at that time, for several reasons. First, there is no real destitution, as there was in the 1930s. There are no soup kitchens. Second, there is a thriving "black" economy (some economists say it amounts to about DM 150 billion a year), which is almost 10 percent of the GNP. Third, present-day unemployment usually affects just one earner in the family, not, as it did back in the 1930s, all earners.

Unemployment will not go away, but there are some hopeful signs. One is that the level of youth unemployment is falling. Another is that new jobs are created by the hundreds and thousands every year: 250,000 last year (1985), roughly 300,000 this year (1986), and we are expecting the same boost in 1987. I think also that in the 1990s demography will come to West Germany's aid and comfort—there will be fewer people entering the work force. In the meantime, it is our task to take care of the older unemployed and to give vocational training to the younger ones because we will need every one of them in the 1990s.

The government can count itself lucky that unemployment does not seem to be a big issue. Not even the Social Democrats have been able to raise it into an issue, nor have the trade unions, which have other problems to battle at the moment. Unemployment is there, we all have compunctions about it, and we all tend to look the other way. But the political process and discussion seem to take place exclusively among those who have a job, and that is one factor that must hold some comfort for the present administration in Bonn.

The January 25, 1987, National Elections

As to the election prospects, I have a few theses. First, Helmut Kohl has it in the bag. The CDU/CSU will be the biggest party again. In fact, there are some people who are now starting to worry that they might poll an absolute majority. I do not think that is probable. It has happened only once—in 1957 when Konrad Adenauer polled an absolute majority—but that also was under different international circumstances. The election was held about nine months after the Hungarian Revolution. Now, if there were elections tomorrow, most pollsters agree that the CDU/CSU would attain a share of 47–48 percent, the Social Democrats a share of 38 percent, and the Liberals and the Greens a share of 7 percent, plus or minus.

I have often said and written back home that Kohl is not an intellectual's politician. He is not, for that matter, a charismatic leader, not a rousing speaker, not a dazzling conceptualizer, and he has an embarassing penchant of putting his foot in his mouth. Gaffs and misspeaks are not the presidential prerogative of Ronald Reagan. But Kohl—and this is a little flag of warning I would like to hoist—knows how to handle power. He knows how to cover his weakest flank. He knows how to work wonders with patronage. He is certainly the toughest survivor we have seen in German politics since Adenauer. Most of his surviving has been done against the bitter onslaught of his Bavarian rival (Franz-Josef Strauss). Kohl has great staying power, and he has been underestimated by some of his critics, including perhaps myself.

He is also a lucky man. The economy is looking up, and with just a little less luck he might not be chancellor today. Had he been put on trial for illegal finance deals on behalf of his party last summer (1985), or had he lost the state elections in Lower Saxony last June (1985), he would quickly have been replaced by the minister of finance, Stoltenberg. But neither event happened; the state prosecutor dropped the case, and Ernst Allbrecht scraped through in Hannover once again. Today Helmut Kohl is firmly in the saddle. There is nobody in his own party to challenge him, not even Franz-Josef Strauss, who has been giving Kohl a lot of flak recently. But not even Strauss is powerful enough to topple the chancellor; Strauss can harass him, but not unseat him. The opposition—and this is the curious feature of this election campaign—somehow just does not figure. Kohl is safe, and some people worry that he might be too safe.

Second, the Social Democrats will be in the wilderness for a long time to come, for a number of different reasons. One is that German politics traditionally moves in long cycles. The CDU was in power for seventeen and one-half years—Adenauer plus Erhard, before the three-year interval of the Grand Coalition. Then there were Social Democratic chancellors for thirteen years. German political culture seems to value stability and abhor frequent shifts, such as are experienced in Italy or Holland.

When the *Machtwechsel* occurred in October 1982, Herbert Wehner, that wise old owl of the Social Democratic party, said, "We'll now be out of power for fifteen years." There were howls of disbelief and protest at the time, but I always thought he was right. My own guess is that the Social Democrats will not be back in power before 1991 or 1995, if they are lucky. That does not necessarily mean that Helmut Kohl will remain chancellor until that time; there might be others from his own party pushing to the top. But I think we will see Christian Democratic chancellors for two more legislative periods.

There are reasons for this. The main reason is that the SPD just is not ready for it. It has been bled white in terms of its program and leadership during its thirteen years in power. The SPD has no convincing slate of leaders to offer today. Johannes Rau is obviously a stopgap, a very nice man, but basically not a fighter. He has described himself as a "fisher of men," but he has not told the fish why they should swallow the bait. Even after most of the campaign is over, it is very hard to tell just what he stands for on any given issue.

The second reason is that the SPD has no convincing program. There are echoes of the past, there is some greenery for decoration, and in fact Willy Brandt, who is an old hand in politics, had the program discussions simply postponed until after the elections. Why? Because it would split the party. By not having this discussion at the moment, he ensures the unity of the party to the extent that this is possible.

There are other reasons that have nothing to do with the quality of the present leadership or with the content of the Social Democratic program. One, for instance, is that the sociological basis of the SPD has been slipping. The party has not come to terms with the new social and sociological givens—especially with the fact that the proportion of blue-collar workers is falling, whereas the proportion of white-collar workers is growing. We are evolving into a service society. The service industry already provides almost 50 percent of the jobs.

The Social Democrats also have an albatross around their neck—their close link with the trade unions, which might amount to the kiss of death at this particular juncture. The unions are in the deepest crisis of their historical existence. They have awakened to the sociological changes in society far too late. They also have on their hands this huge scandal, the Neue Heimat corruption issue, in which the whole philosophy of how trade unions should conduct themselves as a force in the market has been disproved and collapsed in a morass of corruption, incompetence, and sheer blue-eyed naïveté. So people are staying away in droves, and this is one of the problems the Social Democrats will face in January. Many people who would have voted for them some years ago will simply elect to stay home this time.

Rau has put his head valiantly on the chopping block, and it will be chopped off. What his future in German politics is likely to be is hard to say. Maybe he will one day slip into the shoes of Brandt and the chair of the Social Democratic party. The new man or the new men who will leave their imprint on the SPD of the 1990s are still hard to make out. Maybe it will be Oskar Lafontaine, maybe Volker Hauff, maybe Gerhard Schroeder of Hannover. But maybe it will be someone else entirely.

One thing is clear: The Social Democrats will have to move back toward the center before they can win. That there is a lot of leftist or leftist-tinged ideology to their present program simply testifies to their present predicament. They realize full well that it does not matter what they say because they are so far away from power. Some people think, and I even sometimes tend to share their idea, that perhaps the Social Democrats will have to split before they can become an effective political force again, split between real Center-Left Social Democrats and Greens.

Now what about the Greens? My third thesis is that they are probably here to stay. They barged into our parliaments about eight years ago (at the end of the 1970s) and crashed the gate to the Bundestag in 1983. It was quite a thing to see beards in the Bundestag and flowers on the lecterns and no ties! Now the beards are graying; in fact, that is one of their problems. In Hamburg it came to light that in the last elections in November (1985) their representation was greater than average in the age group twenty-five to thirty-five. In fact, there is a distinctly con-servative tinge to the class that is now growing up through the high schools and moving into the universities. The sons are less able; the fifteen-year-old boys who no longer rebelled against their fathers—their liberal fathers—now rebel against their Greenish big brothers, teachers, and young professors.

The Greens were, and to some extent still are, a movement rather than a party. They were basically an "anti" movement: anti–nuclear weapons, anti–civilian nuclear power, anti-industry, anti-pollution, and anti-parliament. Two years ago I thought their political career was already finished. They idolized chaos; they instituted the rotation principle, which means that all their parliamentarians had to give up office after two years, handing it over to totally inexperienced, second-class politicians. They refused any kind of wheeling and dealing, condemning themselves to utter ineffectiveness. They would rather keep their principles pure than taint them by striking compromises. They did not care a hoot about the proprieties of the political process.

Then two things happened. On the one hand, the classical parties stole or absorbed a good deal of the Green program, particularly the Social Democrats, but even the Christian Democrats. On the other hand, a split developed within the Greens, which had been there from the inception but had become a great deal stronger, between action and theory. This split was between what they called the "realos" and the "fundis"—the realists and the fundamentalists. One realist, for instance, is Joschka Fischer, minister of the environment in the state government of Hessen, who is fighting a battle with his own Greens because he still wants to dump poisonous garbage on garbage heaps either in Hessen or in the German Democratic Republic (GDR). Now the city of Hamburg does not want Hessen to dump its stuff in the GDR any longer because Hamburg is only 6 kilometers from the German-German border, and it is likely to spoil the drinking water.

The Greens are still around. In fact, they have been picking up votes. Chernobyl helped, of course. So did the catastrophic chemical spills into the Rhine River a few weeks ago. My guess is that no matter how chaotic their internal constitution, they will be around as long as Chernobyls and Rhine spills and other crimes against the environment happen. I even predict that they will be able to increase their share of the vote on January 25.

My fourth thesis is that the FDP still has a future as the great balancer. To be sure, the liberals have always been an endangered species. But for a while it was next to impossible in West Germany not to be governed by them either in Bonn or in the *Länder*. Their essential role, which is perhaps crucial to the functioning of our system, was not the contribution of a particularly liberal philosophy. Rather, they supplied a modicum of common sense, preventing their partners for the time being from jumping off their respective ideological cliffs. The liberals have done so in coalition with the Social Democrats, and they are now doing this again in coalition with the Christian Democrats. They have often been pronounced dead, but actually each time this happened, it was the surest sign that they would be resuscitated again. Whenever they are pronounced dead, people say, "Well we wouldn't really want to do without them." They hover around 4.7 percent two days before election Sunday, and then they come out with 7.5 percent or even more.

The interesting feature about the present election campaign is the following: The really rough and rude and vital exchanges do not take place between the government coalition and the opposition. They take place within the coalition, especially between the right wing of the CDU/CSU and the FDP. The right-wingers feel that the liberals exert an influence on government policy far beyond the weight of their numbers—they dropped the fight against terrorism and asylum seekers; they pushed for too much détente to the East (that is one thing for which the Foreign Office and its present chief are particularly being attacked); they are too ready for disarmament measures; they are beastly to the white South Africans; they plead for West Germany's export of weapons to the Third World; and they are far too inhibited by Germany's Nazi past. The fight between Franz-Josef Strauss and Hans-Dietrich Genscher is on and will prove the dominant feature of the election campaign.

There have often been complaints about the *Nebenaussenpolitik*, a "parallel foreign policy" conducted by the Social Democrats. But the real *Nebenaussenpolitik* is now being conducted by the CSU. One might almost say that this is *counter*–foreign policy rather than a *Neben*–foreign policy, threatening to break up the domestic consensus about Germany's role in the world.

Foreign Policy After Reykjavik

German foreign policy is based on some very sound principles. First, there is the U.S. connection, which is important and will remain so. Second, there is the European hope. Europe has become a kind of "ersatz fatherland," a substitute for German national ambitions, a vessel in which we can live out our national destiny and a framework in which we feel contained—*aufgehoben* in the threefold Hegelian sense of the term: uplifted, contained (hemmed in), and preserved. Third, there is a necessity to do business with the Soviets and the rest of Eastern Europe. Fourth, there is a deeply ingrained desire to keep things on an even keel with East Germany, and fifth, there is a desire to play a useful role in the development of the Third World. I think these are the basic elements; I will not go into them.

Anti-Americanism?

I will address myself to two or three questions. First, is anti-Americanism rampant in Germany? I think it is not. The Federal Republic came into being under the protective umbrella of the United States; it owes its survival through manifold crises to the United States; and it still depends on its great transatlantic ally. Détente has not yet reached the point where the iron necessity of securing our existence has let up, and this will remain so. The U.S. connection remains the foundation of West German security.

Now, having said this, I would add that perhaps there will no longer be total congruence of interests. We have become economic rivals in many respects. We have our own view on the West's policy vis-à-vis the East. We have strategic ideas that are not always in congruence with those that happen to be in fashion at the Pentagon. But we also have doubts about the reliability of the United States that are nourished by a certain fear that the United States is being pulled away from Europe by the lure of "Asia, the continent of the twenty-first century." Some people are worried about a renewal of U.S. isolationism in the guise of unilateralism. Others are worried by a certain unsteadiness in the U.S. political system: with the exception of the current president, a system of one-term presidents since Dwight Eisenhower; quite abrupt changes in policy each time a new president assumes office; a continual seesaw between the administration and the legislative branch; and an internal rivalry between the National Security Council and the State Department.

Now there are many who are wondering whether we are in for another two years of U.S. paralysis, whether Reagan is another president whose mythology crumbles before his term expires. To be frank, in Germany we perhaps did not wake up to this crisis as quickly as we should have. Comparing German newspapers and, for instance, British newspapers, it struck me that it took the German newspapers about ten days longer than the British newspapers to pick up this theme and to see the danger that we will now have a president hobbled for the rest of his tenure and a United States preoccupied with yet another investigation, with yet another scandal. I think it has been dawning on us in the meantime that although we hope and wish that the U.S. people can sort out this sordid affair, we are also worried about the capacity of the president to act and about the effectiveness of the apparatus that runs his foreign policy.

The point I am trying to make here is that these doubts do not constitute anti-Americanism. Where it does exist, it is not a mass phenomenon; it is statistically almost invisible; and all serious polls—Allensbach, Emnid, Infas—agree that U.S. popularity is undiminished and that it has more or less remained constant at about 66 percent during the past forty years or so. Similar figures for other West European countries indicate that anti-Americanism is much less rampant in West Germany than it is, for instance, in France or in Britain.

Arms Control

The second question I would like to raise in this context concerns arms control. How did we react to Reykjavik, inasmuch as there was a studied, informed, and considered reaction? Let me remind you of one basic fact. The two Germanys have the largest concentration of military power anywhere in the world. There are close to 1 million troops in West Germany; there are about 400,000 troops in uniform in East Germany. There are about 4,000 nuclear weapons in West Germany, 1,700 launchers for these weapons, and 100 special ammunition sites dotting the country. In East Germany, there are about 3,500 nuclear weapons with about 1,500 launchers. There is an inherent interest in arms control and disarmament in Germany because of this concentration of military power, because of the dangers inherent in them, and because of the simple geographical fact that, if ever worse came to worst, Germany would be the battlefield. We realize that building up military strength is necessary, but it is not sufficient to obtain security. Winding down the arms race and creating economic and societal stability are just as important.

For this reason, the Germans want the Reykjavik approach of fewer nuclear weapons to succeed, although perhaps not in all its ramifications. In fact, many of us were equally worried by the two conflicting and colliding visions of a totally nuclear-free world, one propounded by President Reagan in March 1983 and the other by General Secretary Mikhail Gorbachev last January (1986). We think that there has to be a minimum deterrent left over at the end of the day that ensures against miscalculation. Some in the United States argue, "Well, you simply do that because you are afraid to field the conventional armies that it would then take." It is not possible to field them. We have not got the men; the pool of draft-age men will be getting smaller and smaller. We have not got the money, and the best way to address this problem is to get the Soviets to draw their conventional strength down, not to talk ourselves into building up our conventional strength. It goes without saying that we would be afraid of a world in which the United States had totally divested itself of nuclear weapons.

We would be very much in favor of a first step, even as large a step as a 50 percent reduction, which they talked about in Reykjavik. Then we will see what will follow after that, whether inspection will work, whether verification can be trusted. Then we can see how far the process will go. I myself would not believe for a moment that the two superpowers, having emptied their nuclear arsenals by 90 percent, would then go ahead and take out the last 10 percent as well, leaving France and China as the supreme nuclear powers in the world. I think at best we will move toward a world minimum-deterrent force.

We would like to make a start in the field of medium-range missiles. There were some stray noises out of Bonn and elsewhere, but it is simply inconceivable to me that our governments tell the people for five or six years that the dual-track decision means either that we arm upward, or we reduce if the Soviets reduce. If they are ready to reduce, and if they are ready to reduce to zero, we cannot now say we never meant that we'd agree to zero. Anyway, I think many of the reasons given for the deployment of these weapons were specious in the first place, and this problem has to be tackled. At the same time, we have to start talking about reducing those shorter-range/medium-range arsenals that were introduced after the implementation of the double-track decision.

But we should not talk ourselves into another *Nachrüstung*, saying that if the Soviets do not draw down their capabilities in that particular sector, we will have to build up to their strength. This is something, for instance, that Franz-Josef Strauss has been propounding recently. We are in favor of continued U.S. observance of the Strategic Arms Limitation Talks II treaty. We do not want a U.S. breakout of the Antiballistic Missile treaty. We favor deep cuts at least to the 50 percent threshold. We favor the zero-zero solution in Europe and talks about shorter-range reductions and about conventional reduction.

The German National Question

The final question is this: Are the Germans bolting the Western stable simply because of their national question, their national problem? I think the Germans have learned their lessons. They have learned, for instance, that historical claims can be forfeited. They have learned that deeply held national aspirations are subject to change. My father marched into Austria because it was thought inconceivable that Austria was not part of Germany. Now we live in good-neighborly relations with the Austrians, and the *Anschluss* (annexation) debate is as dead as the dodo. A similar thing might happen in the relationship between West Germany and East Germany.

Of course, reunification is still in our statute books. Reunification is still something that we would like to happen. But it is not part of our operative foreign policy. It is something we leave to the tides of history, knowing full well that the tides of history may not work in our favor and also realizing that there are in our history other models of German-German coexistence than that of Otto von Bismarck's unitarian state. If an accommodation were ever reached between East and West that would make reunification possible, unity would probably then be superfluous. It is not so much the fact that we are divided that grates and hurts. It is rather the quality of this division that troubles us, and if that quality can be changed over time—and this is a long-term process at best—then I think the issue of reunification might die away as the issue of *Anschluss* has died away.

Conclusion

I will leave it at this, limiting myself perhaps to saying that on the whole, there are three sorts of politicians: those who make events happen, those who watch events happen, and those who wonder what happened. We do not have any in Germany or elsewhere in Europe who make events happen. There is no genius for architectonics around; and we are not governed by men or women of a stature comparable to that of founding fathers Robert Schumann, Konrad Adenauer, Alcide DeGasperi, Charles de Gaulle, and Winston Churchill.

As for Germany, one might even call it lucky that it does not need any greater men because its problems are so small and there is no necessity. On the whole I think we are a normal country, and if this normalcy is nothing very heroic, then it is also nothing that ought to cause us to lie awake at night. I look to the future with a reasonable degree of confidence. I feel myself rather in the position of the wise man who was asked whether he considered himself an optimist or a pessimist? He said, "I guess I'm an optimist." The other said, "If you're an optimist, why do you scowl?" He said, "Well, I don't quite trust my judgment!"

The Role of Germany Within NATO and Europe

Horst Teltschik

Parameters of German Foreign Policy

The Federal Republic of Germany (FRG) is affected more strongly than other countries by international structures and processes. Owing to the country's location in the middle of Europe, the question of to whom Germany belongs and where the Germans belong has explosive potential at both the European and the global level. For three hundred years, Germany has been closely tied to the European power structure. V. I. Lenin once said that control of Germany means control of Europe and that the path to Europe is through Berlin. Our European neighbors in the West, especially France, carefully record—like seismographs—political tremors that might indicate a change in Germany's external orientation.

Furthermore, the Federal Republic of Germany lacks raw materials and hence, as an industrial nation, is highly dependent on imports of major raw materials from all parts of the world—up to 100 percent in some key sectors. In 1986, we became the world's main exporter. With an export rate of 35 percent, one in every three jobs in the Federal Republic of Germany depends on exports. Our economic dependence on the rest of the world is thus self-evident. At the same time, we realize that we cannot permanently retain our high standards of achievement in research and technology if we rely solely on our own resources. Top-level achievements on a global scale increasingly call for an intensive

This speech was given to the Annual Conference of the Robert Bosch Foundation Alumni Association, September 26, 1987, Washington, D.C. Introductory remarks were given by the Minister of the Embassy of the Federal Republic of Germany, Karl Th. Paschke.

exchange of scientific and technological know-how with the leading industrial nations of the free world. It is therefore not surprising that, especially in recent years, this international cooperation at the bilateral and multilateral levels has been considerably expanded.

These examples from the economic, scientific, and technological spheres show that many domestic problems and challenges can now be solved only in an international context. This also applies to such areas as environmental protection, energy conservation, and the combating of terrorism. This is also true for both superpowers and is one reason Mikhail Gorbachev has to seek more international cooperation on all levels. Domestic policy and foreign policy are becoming ever more interdependent. Most Germans have not yet realized this or do not want to accept it. What else could explain the persistent, widespread tendency toward national introversion in the Federal Republic of Germany, when openness, dialogue, and cooperation on a global scale are needed. Some partners abroad even suspect the Germans want to persist in a state of self-satisfaction or even self-righteousness and create an island of prosperity in order to avoid international responsibility, even though it has long been in their own interest to accept it.

This situation is all the more disquieting considering the international developments that have affected Germany since 1945. The bipolarity of the two superpowers, the United States and the Soviet Union, is reflected more directly and strikingly in Germany than anywhere else. The border between the two social systems cuts through the middle of Germany and divides a free democracy from a Communist one-party dictatorship. These are two mutually antagonistic social systems that each side considers incompatible, like "fire and water," as General Secretary Erich Honecker said during his visit in Bonn in September 1987.

This divided status quo is part of the overall European setup. Many feel a change in this setup would pose a threat to the peace in Europe that has prevailed for more than forty years. Therefore, the overcoming of the division of Germany and hence of Europe must be sought by peaceful means. It will be attainable only through cooperation with all neighbors in West and East, not through confrontation with them.

These premises are indispensable because for forty years nuclear weapons have largely determined the system of strategic stability between West and East. Armed conflict would be tantamount to disaster, particularly for Europeans. Nevertheless, Europeans know that our freedom and security are only guaranteed as long as we are protected by the nuclear umbrella and the military presence of the United States and our allies. German foreign and security policy must therefore remain embedded in the web formed by the North Atlantic Treaty Organization (NATO) and free Europe.

Basic Political Decisions Taken in Germany Since 1949

Given this complex network of dependence and interlinkage of German policy, and in view of the bitter experience gained in two world wars and during Adolf Hitler's dictatorship, the Germans drew these clear-cut conclusions after 1945:

- Germans want to live in peace—never again war!

- Germans want to live in freedom—no Fascist or Communist dictatorship!

- Germans want to live in a democracy. Pluralism and the rule of law, human dignity and tolerance must form the basis of society.

- Germans seek economic prosperity and social justice. Only social harmony guarantees domestic peace, which is the prerequisite for external peace.

After 1945, there was only one chance of reaching and maintaining these goals for the free part of Germany: the integration of the Federal Republic of Germany into the free world, into the community of shared values formed by the free democracies of the United States and Europe. The decisions that Konrad Adenauer made then remain irreversible for the current government headed by the Christian Democratic Union (CDU) and the Christian Social Union (CSU):

- Close friendship and partnership on equal terms with the United States are the guarantees of our freedom and security.

- The North Atlantic Alliance and the European Community (EC) are the foundations of our defense capacity and of our policy for peace and understanding with all our neighbors in the West and the East.

- A socially tempered market economy and a free world economy guarantee the economic development of our country and the social security of our citizens.

German Foreign Policy Options

The FRG as an Economic Power

The Federal Republic of Germany has attained significant standing in the world economy by virtue of its economic strength and the high level it has attained in science and technology, education and training, and social security. These achievements were the prerequisite and foundation of a stable democratic system, which has proved its worth for almost forty years. As a result, the Federal Republic of Germany enjoys a high reputation and has a strong appeal worldwide. The FRG is the most important U.S. partner in the alliance, the main partner in the European Community, and a much sought-after partner for Eastern and Third World countries. The FRG's economic and political stability remains its chief asset and enables the country to pursue national interests as an equal, full-fledged partner of the international community. The more successful we are at home, the greater the scope for influence abroad.

President François Mitterrand of France has pointed out that France and the Federal Republic of Germany together have a population of 110 million. If the economic and technological potential of the two countries were combined and joint use made of the high level of education and training of the people, the common achievements would be greater than those of the Soviet Union. Such a vision has many interesting prospects.

Friendship with the United States

The current governing coalition in the FRG is repeatedly accused of being too submissive to the policies of the U.S. government. But the FRG government is an equal, self-assured ally. Never before have the bilateral and multilateral consultations been as close and wide-ranging as they are today. Chancellor Helmut Kohl is a close friend of President Ronald Reagan. All of this helps to strengthen and safeguard the opportunities for exercising influence on, and having a say in, the actions of the United States.

What would be gained if the FRG government, for the sake of confirming its independence, were to seek public confrontation with its U.S. partner for no justifiable reason? Bonn would no doubt be immediately wooed by Moscow, without gaining any greater weight or influence there. On the contrary, the Soviet Union would immediately try to exploit differences between the Federal Republic of Germany and the United States for its own purposes in order to break up the solidarity of the Western alliance. We would become a pawn of Soviet policies.

In actual fact, close friendship with the United States increases our weight not only in Washington but also in Moscow. This may appear paradoxical at first glance. But the Soviet leaders realize all too well that it serves their interests if the federal government is able to exercise influence on U.S. policies—if it helps to expound German and European interests in Washington and to incorporate them in U.S., as well as Soviet, decisions. The fact that the dialogue between the two superpowers has again gotten under way in recent years, that summit meetings between President Reagan and General Secretary Gorbachev have become possible, and that substantive disarmament and arms control proposals have been placed on the negotiating tables is due in no small measure to the FRG government having taken rigorous action and launched initiatives of its own in Washington and in the alliance. The Soviet Union also realizes that we can expedite or slow down this process. But it is not prepared to concede that this close partnership with the United States precludes cooperation between the Federal Republic of Germany and the Soviet Union. On the contrary, this partnership frees German policies toward the East of any dubiousness, widens the scope for them, and makes the federal government a predictable and reliable partner for both sides.

This also applies with respect to the countries of the Third World. They do not expect the Federal Republic of Germany to act as intermediary or arbiter in regional troublespots, such as the Middle East, southern Africa, or Central America. They have long abandoned such illusions, if they ever had them. These countries, however, are aware of the FRG government's close friendship with the U.S. government and of the weight that Bonn carries in Washington. It is in their interest to take advantage of this fact and to gain our support for their concerns. This is also in our own interest because it is proof of the trust placed in the Federal Republic of Germany and also because, often enough, it constitutes the only way for us to make a constructive contribution toward the solution of conflicts in the Third World.

Stability of the Western Alliance

When Chancellor Helmut Kohl assumed office in 1982, one of his declared objectives was to strengthen the cohesion of the Western Alliance and to live up to West Germany's obligations. The Federal Republic of Germany possesses the strongest conventional army in Western Europe and is thus the main European pillar of NATO. This determines our weight in the alliance and our influence on the common policies pursued.

But Germans should bear in mind that our newly acquired military strength and our political weight are tolerable to our European allies only because the Federal Republic of Germany and the Bundeswehr are fully integrated into the political and military structures of NATO. This integration guarantees security for us and our European allies as well as security for our Western partners against us. This is the basis of a considerable part of the trust that our Western friends have in our policies. Whoever questions or seeks to reverse this integration will destroy this trust, create insecurity and distrust, and harm German interests.

The interdependence within the alliance does not restrict our room for maneuver but widens it, not least in our relations with the East. With our anchor in the North Atlantic Alliance, which guarantees our security, we have the necessary cover to pursue an active policy of understanding and cooperation with our Eastern neighbors.

European Integration

The United States and Canada form one abutment of the Atlantic bridge, whereas the European Community forms the other. The latter still has to go a long way to become a political and economic unity. With a total population of 320 million, the EC will constitute the world's largest internal market by 1992, if this goal of one internal market can be attained by then. Its economic appeal in Europe and worldwide is already evident.

Cooperation among the members of the European Community in foreign and security policy is still rudimentary. But even at this stage, such cooperation could considerably increase the influence and weight of the Europeans vis-à-vis the two world powers. Examples already exist of progress and results achieved through joint initiatives by European governments or by the community as a whole, launched in Washington or in East-West negotiations. The Federal Republic of Germany and France form the core of this community. Cooperation between these two countries is, as it were, a fundamental law of any European policy and serves German interests and those of the European Community as a whole.

By speaking out strongly and unequivocally in favor of the NATO two-track decision in the German Bundestag in 1983, President Mitterrand strengthened the FRG government's position at home and vis-à-vis its Soviet adversary. The close Franco-German coordination and cooperation in the European Community have permitted major progress to be made, particularly during 1982–1987. President Mitterrand described the value of this cooperation most cogently when he referred publicly in Paris and Bonn to the existence of a Franco-German community of fate. (This utterance by a French president was hardly a matter of course, although it was not taken up by the German media.)

The French writer Leon Bloy once said, "If France suffers, then God suffers." Bearing in mind these words, Chancellor Helmut Kohl developed a close rapport with the French president and energetically advanced their relationship. President Mitterrand and Chancellor Kohl have set a world record by meeting more than fifty times from 1982 to 1987. Nevertheless, political decisions require more than friendship and mutual trust. If concrete results are to be achieved, common interests must exist.

In the years of Helmut Kohl's chancellorship (1982–1987), substantive progress has been made in three areas within the European Community and in bilateral relations with France:

- At the Milan Summit of the European Community in mid-1985, Bonn and Paris jointly presented a draft treaty on cooperation in foreign and security policy. In December 1985, this draft became the basis for a decision by all twelve member states. In addition, the internal market is to be completed by 1992.

- The West German government and the French government laid the foundations for the European technological community known as EUREKA. After two years, EUREKA embraced 170 high-tech projects in the amount of DM 9 billion for joint European space research in the Columbus, Ariane V, and HERMES projects and for a joint European aviation industry based on the Airbus family as a counterbalance to the cooperation between the U.S. and Japanese aviation industries.

- In February 1986, Chancellor Kohl and President Mitterrand agreed to expand and intensify considerably the bilateral cooperation in defense and security policy that had been agreed on by Konrad Adenauer and Charles de Gaulle in 1963 when they signed the German-French treaty of friendship.

- President Mitterrand became the first French president to agree to consultation procedures for the use of prestrategic nuclear weapons on German soil. This step, which Helmut Schmidt and Willy Brandt constantly sought but never achieved, has been the result of the close rapport between Helmut Kohl and François Mitterrand.

- Operative cooperation between the German Armed Forces and the First French Army and the French Rapid Deployment Force is being intensified. Cooperation between the armed forces will occur at all levels in the future. In 1986 and 1987, joint maneuvers were held for the first time at the level of major formations (involving 75,000 troops in 1987).

- The general staff officers are to receive joint training after their national training courses.

When Helmut Kohl and President Mitterrand visited the largest bilateral German-French battle maneuver in East Bavaria, on September 24, 1987, both decided to create a joint defense council. This will institutionalize their cooperation on the military level and intensify their operative cooperation by building up united military forces such as the common brigade Chancellor Kohl already announced. As President Mitterrand said, Germany and France want to pave the way for a new European joint security structure. Other West European countries could adhere later on; some are already interested.

This policy is not aimed against the United States or against NATO. The opposite is true. We want to strengthen the European pillar of the alliance. The magnitude of these steps between Germany and France can only be appreciated by those who recall 1914 and 1939 as well as the fact that there have been twenty-seven major wars between Germany and France since 1519, when Charles V acceded to the throne. Helmut Kohl is the first German chancellor to succeed in developing productive, friendly relations with the United States and its president and with France and its president. There is no longer any dispute between those who favored a Gaullist policy and those who advocated an Atlantic course. This is an asset that we must exploit as long as it is available.

International Responsibility of the Western Europeans

It is time to expand and intensify this Franco-German and European cooperation at all levels. Those who keep complaining that Europeans are not consulted by the United States in its decisions and actions concerning foreign and security policy, but have to share liability all too quickly, must ask themselves this: When do Europeans assume international responsibility, and what is their contribution toward containing and managing international or regional crises?

If there is an increasing number of people in the United States who favor easing the U.S. military burden and reducing U.S. forces in Europe, it will not be possible in the longer run to reverse this trend by vociferous complaints. Instead, Europeans must develop our own alternatives for adequately guaranteeing our security in future.

If the two superpowers investigate and develop new strategic systems, they will not be dissuaded by a strongly voiced "no" from their European partners. Europeans realize, however, that our own vital security interests are directly affected by this. That is why we, too, must consider what shape such a new system of strategic stability should ultimately take so as to avoid being decoupled from the security of the United States.

If we want to ensure that we do not continue responding so helplessly to military actions by the United States, as in the cases of Grenada and Libya, we must develop common foreign policy instruments of our own that enable us to assume greater international responsibility and to achieve a sensible form of burden sharing with our U.S. partner. As long as the twelve members of the European Community act—or rather react—solely through written declarations on the narrow basis of the smallest common denominator, they will not impress the superpowers or any other country in the world. In the light of these considerations, close cooperation among the free countries of Europe, pursued in a spirit of friendship at all levels, could offer strong prospects for more stable peace and for freedom, security, and prosperity on our continent and far beyond.

Policy of Dialogue and Cooperation with the East

The integration of the Federal Republic of Germany into the Western Alliance and the European Community forms the solid foundation of German foreign policy. This strong anchor affords us scope to pursue our own policy of détente with the East.

When the CDU/CSU/FDP coalition took the reins in 1982, the government's declared aim was to develop relations with all Warsaw Pact countries at all levels. The failure of the intermediate-range nuclear forces (INF) disarmament talks in Geneva in 1983 confirmed the FRG government's conviction that results in the field of disarmament and arms control are only attainable if political relations are simultaneously developed. Disarmament and arms control are one of the most difficult and complex tasks of West-East relations. They therefore require a very large degree of mutual trust. How can results be attained if political relations are stagnant or even frozen?

How much room for maneuver does the Federal Republic of Germany possess in the context of West-East relations? Experience shows that the development of relations between the two superpowers is a decisive prerequisite for increasing the latitude of the respective European partners in West and East. This applies particularly to the two German states. When General Secretary Erich Honecker attempted in 1983 and 1984, despite the start of U.S. INF deployments in Europe, to continue and intensify his policy of dialogue and cooperation, which was contrary to Soviet instructions, Moscow vetoed his intention to visit Bonn in September 1984. This episode was a highly visible demonstration of the limits of the GDR's maneuverability. It was not until three years later, in September 1987, that Honecker was able to carry out his visit.

It is therefore in our own interest to keep the process of understanding between the two superpowers going. But it cannot be our task to assume the role of an intermediary or arbiter between them. We are not Atlas, who could bear the superpowers on his shoulders and bring them together. In the final analysis, they do not need any intermediary if they want to speak to one another. Our task can only be to exert influence in Washington and seek a dialogue with Moscow so as to maintain relations between West and East, introduce ideas, and solicit support for dialogue and cooperation. This was Chancellor Kohl's motive in November 1982 in Washington and in July 1983 in his talks with General Secretary Yuri Andropov, when he urged that a summit meeting be held. The successful results of the summits in Geneva and Reykjavik bear out this position. The most extensive disarmament and arms control proposals have been tabled in all areas: nuclear, conventional, and chemical weapon systems. Diverse talks are also being held between the superpowers on regional troublespots, human rights, and economic cooperation.

The federal government has actively participated from the outset in this process of West-East dialogue with strong initiatives of its own at the bilateral and multilateral levels and has sought close coordination and consultation with its European partners, with the United States, and within the alliance. The FRG has also carefully examined all Soviet proposals. It has taken up in a constructive manner the positive elements of the Soviet proposals and tried to make use of them for the purpose of achieving progress.

The federal government has simultaneously sought to develop and intensify its bilateral relations with the Soviet Union. But after the start of the deployment of U.S. INF missiles, the Soviet leaders could not resist the temptation of initiating a policy aimed at politically isolating the Federal Republic of Germany. This attempt was contradictory to General Secretary Gorbachev's subsequent pursuit of a policy vis-à-vis Western Europe based on the concept of a common European house. Such a concept would be doomed to failure from the start if the FRG were excluded. This rough time seems to be over. We expect a visit from Foreign Secretary Edvard Shevardnadze in Bonn this fall (1987) to prepare for the meeting between Chancellor Kohl and General Secretary Gorbachev. In this regard, Kohl's decision not to modernize the German Pershing IA missiles, but to dismantle them, was crucial for the U.S.-Soviet INF negotiations in Washington in September 1987 and for improving West German–Soviet relations.

Outlook

German foreign policy remains a web of sovereign opportunities and international dependence. These constitute factors of strength and of weakness. It is up to us to mobilize all our resources and take advantage of all opportunities in order to expand our foreign policy options and increase their weight. What Germans need are more imagination and creativity as well as the ability to play a role of our own in international affairs. We need more courage in shouldering international responsibility, less introversion, less ideology, less moral severity toward others, and more rationality and realism. We cannot regard ourselves as an isle of bliss that is not affected by the storms of the general political climate or is able to remain aloof from the frictions of international politics.

West German Federal Governments and Chancellors Since 1949

Year	Government	Chancellor
1949	CDU/CSU/FDP*	Konrad Adenauer
1953	CDU/CSU/FDP*	Konrad Adenauer
1957	CDU/CSU	Konrad Adenauer
1961	CDU/CSU/FDP	Konrad Adenauer
1963	CDU/CSU/FDP	Ludwig Erhard
1965	CDU/CSU/FDP	Ludwig Erhard
1966	CDU/CSU/SPD	Kurt Georg Kiessinger
1969	SPD/FDP	Willy Brandt
1972	SPD/FDP	Willy Brandt
1974	SPD/FDP	Helmut Schmidt
1976	SPD/FDP	Helmut Schmidt
1980	SPD/FDP	Helmut Schmidt
1982	CDU/CSU/FDP	Helmut Kohl
1983	CDU/CSU/FDP	Helmut Kohl
1987	CDU/CSU/FDP	Helmut Kohl

* Several smaller parties also participated in the 1949 and 1953 coalition governments.

The CDU does not campaign in Bavaria, leaving the field to the CSU, which in turn does not campaign nationally. At the federal level, the two parties form one joint parliamentary block in the Bundestag.

About the Contributors

Daniel J. Broderick graduated with distinction in political science from Stanford University. In 1979 he received his law degree from Yale University, where he was a member of the board of editors of the *Yale Law Journal*. He served as an assistant U.S. attorney in Los Angeles, California, for four years. As a Bosch Fellow in 1985–1986 he worked with the North Rhine–Westphalia Ministry for Economics, Small Business, and Technology and with Thyssen Steel, Duisberg. He is now an associate professor of law at Pepperdine University School of Law, Malibu, California.

Edwina S. Campbell was a Fulbright Fellow at the University of Freiburg and received her Ph.D. from the Fletcher School of Law and Diplomacy in 1982. She is a former foreign service officer and assistant professor of government and foreign affairs at the University of Virginia. She has also been the recipient of travel grants from the American Council on Germany, the German Marshall Fund, and the Stiftung für die deutsche Wissenschaft. As a Bosch Fellow in 1985–1986 she was in the German Parliament and the Foreign Office. She is currently a senior research analyst at Eagle Research Group, Arlington, Virginia.

Karin L. Johnston received her B.A. from the University of Nebraska and M.A. from the Graduate School of International Studies, University of Denver (1985). She has served as staff assistant to the lieutenant governor of Colorado (1982–1985) and as a coordinator at the Center for International Security Studies at the University of Maryland. During the Bosch Fellowship in 1985–1986, Johnston was assigned to the Federal Ministry for Inner-German Relations in Bonn and to the State Agency for Assistance in Berlin. She is presently pursuing a Ph.D. in security studies at the University of Maryland.

David R. Larrimore holds a bachelor of chemical engineering from Georgia Institute of Technology (1975) and an MBA from Stanford (1985). His work experience includes production engineering with ITT Rayonier and both research and marketing positions with Dow Chemical, USA, from 1975 to 1983. His internship as a Bosch Fellow in 1985–1986 was with the Federal Ministry of Research and Technology in Bonn and with Siemens AG/Techno Venture Management in Munich. In 1986 he rejoined McKinsey & Co., San Francisco, California, and has consulted in international and technology management studies.

Kathryn S. Mack received her B.A. in history from Cornell University and J.D. from Yale Law School. She served as a law clerk to the Supreme Court of the Federated States of Micronesia. As a Bosch Fellow in 1985–1986 she spent three months at the Federal Ministry for Inner-German Relations and three months at the West Berlin Ministry of Economics. She is currently an associate, specializing in international finance, at a major New York law firm.

Gale A. Mattox received a Ph.D. from the Woodrow Wilson School, University of Virginia (1981). She has been an international relations analyst with Congressional Research Service (1974–1976), a Fulbright scholar (1978–1979), NATO Research Fellow (1984–1986), and International Affairs Fellow, Council on Foreign Relations, at the State Department's Office of Strategic and Theater Nuclear Policy (1985–1986). As a Bosch Fellow in 1984–1985, she was with the German Defense Ministry and in the Office of the Governor, Northrhine-Westfalia. She is an associate professor of political science at the U.S. Naval Academy, Annapolis, Maryland. Mattox has published a number of articles and co-edited with Catherine McArdle Kelleher, *Evolving European Defense Policies* (1987).

Dennis P. McLaughlin earned his B.S. in chemical engineering from the University of Arizona and a J.D. from Stanford Law School in 1983. He worked for the Maricopa County attorney in Phoenix, Arizona, from 1983 to 1986, prosecuting felony cases. As a Bosch Fellow in 1986–1987 he worked with the First Criminal Senate of the Federal Supreme Court, Karlsruhe, and with the Office of the State Prosecutor, Stuttgart. He is presently a lawyer in the firm of Miller & Pitt, Tucson, Arizona, practicing in the areas of commercial and personal injury litigation.

Sandra E. Peterson graduated magna cum laude from Cornell University. In 1987 she received an M.P.A. from the Woodrow Wilson School, Princeton University, where she was a Woodrow Wilson Fellow. Her professional experience includes specialist assistant, American Stock Exchange; consultant, Multinational Strategies, Inc.; and Rapporteur, Council on Foreign Relations. She was in charge of Science, Technology and Public Policy Program Development at Princeton University from

1986 to 1987. As a Bosch Fellow in 1984–1985 she was with the Federal Ministry for Finance and the Federation of German Industries, Cologne. She is now an associate with McKinsey & Company, Inc., Stamford, Connecticut.

Barbara A. Reeves holds a B.A. in German and political science and a J.D. from Wayne State University in Detroit (1982). She served as law clerk to the Michigan Supreme Court in 1983–1984 and 1985–1986 and was a member of the board of directors of the Council Against Domestic Assault in Lansing. While on the Bosch Fellowship in 1984–1985, she worked in the women's policy sections of both the Family Ministry in Bonn and the Family Senate in Berlin and at the First Autonomous Shelter in Berlin. In 1986 she returned to Berlin and worked full time at the shelter until mid-1987. She currently works as a legal editor in Berlin.

A. Bradley Shingleton received an M.T.S. from Harvard University and a J.D. from Duke University School of Law in 1982. He was an associate with Young, Moore, Henderson, and Alvis in Raleigh, North Carolina, from 1982 to 1986. As a Bosch Fellow in 1986–1987, he served with the Federal Ministry of Justice and the Robert Bosch GmbH in Gerlingen. He served as president of the Robert Bosch Foundation Alumni Association in 1987–1988. Shingleton is an associate with the law firm of Walter, Conston, Alexander & Green, P.C., New York City.

Theo Sommer studied in Sweden, Tübingen University, and the University of Chicago. His doctoral dissertation, "Germany and Japan Between the Powers, 1935–1940," was published in 1962. He was a reader for political science at the University of Hamburg from 1967 to 1970. Sommer became foreign editor of *Die Zeit* in 1958 and deputy editor in 1968. He was chief of the planning staff, Ministry of Defense, Bonn, 1969–1970. He is author and editor of several books—most recently, *The Chinese Card* (1979), *Changing Alliance?* (1982), *Look Back into the Future* (1984), *Travel to the Other Germany* (1986)—and is a frequent contributor to U.S. publications such as *Foreign Affairs* and *Newsweek International*. He is a member of the Council of the International Institute for Strategic Studies (London), the Steering Committee of the Bildeberg Meetings, and the Trilateral Commission. He holds an honorary doctorate of law, University of Maryland. He has been editor in chief of *Die Zeit* since 1973.

Horst Teltschik studied political science, modern history, and international law at the Free University of Berlin, completing a degree in political science in 1967. His professional experience includes research assistant at Otto Suhr Institute, Free University; head of the CDU Office Foreign and German Policy Section; assistant secretary in the State Chancellery of Rhineland-Palatinate; and office director of the CDU/ CSU Parliamentary Party Chair. Since October 1982, Teltschik has served as head of the Directorate-General for Foreign and Intra-German Relations, Development Policy and External Security in the Federal Chancellory, and since 1983, he has served also as deputy head of the Chancellory, Bonn.

John H. Vaughan, Jr. received his B.A. from Northwestern University and J.D. from Santa Clara University. He interned at the U.N. Law of the Sea Conference (1976–1977) and at the Informationszentrum, Berlin (1977). From 1977 to 1986, he was a staff attorney at the Foreign Claims Settlement Commission, U.S. Department of Justice. As a Bosch Fellow in 1986–1987, Vaughan served at the Ministry for Inner-German Relations and with the Senator for Economics in Berlin. He subsequently served as law clerk to a judge at the U.S. Claims Court, Washington, D.C., and is currently an attorney with the Representative for German Industry and Trade, also in Washington, D.C.

Index